A JOURNEY OF

CLARITY

8 Practices to Attain Clarity

ANA DIEZ

Cover design and illustration: Natasha Pierre-Louis and Peter Jison
Back cover photograph: Monica Ramirez

Library of Congress Cataloging-in-Publication Data

Diez, Ana

A Journey of Clarity: 8 Practices to Attain Clarity
ISBN 978-0-615-57371-7
1. Self-Help 2. Spirituality
TXu 1-776-170   2011

ISBN 978-0-615-57371-7
Printed in the United States of America
Distributed by CreateSpace

Ana Maria, your profound wisdom and love toward life have supported my journey. You inspire my actions. The way in which you move through every situation reminds me of how effortless life can be when lived from a place of kindness and compassion. You are the most remarkable soul I have encountered and feel forever grateful to be your daughter.

Andres, it has been a joy to share life with you. Witnessing your growth everyday is an incredible gift. Your enthusiasm to experiencing life fully and your capacity to be grounded are extraordinary. I thank you for your constant words of love and encouragement. With the deepest love, Mom.

We are not here to suffer but to become more conscious. We are here to create balance between our humanity and our spirituality. We are here to obtain clarity and make choices that match a purpose. We are here to heal ourselves and others.

We are here to BE at peace within.

Ana Diez

CONTENTS

ACKNOWLEDGMENTS

To my mother, Ana Maria, and my father, Roberto, for raising me. You have always allowed me space to Be, respected me and believed in me. This book would have not come into existence without your encouragement and unconditional love. I could not have wished for better parents.

To my son, Andres, for the time spent together, for being a source of strength, for your amazing personality and your extraordinary capacity to adapt to change. You enhance my life with so much joy. I love you.

To my two brothers, Roberto and Luis, for your support and love. I admire your perseverance and your positive outlook in life. Thank you for teaching me how to be a better sister.

To Charlie, for allowing me to love your beautiful soul. No words can express the gratitude I feel for the support and nurturing I have received from you through the years. Thank you for providing me with so many opportunities to grow as a person, and for the love you have given me. I feel honored to have met you.

To Genevieve, Margarita, Alexandra, Monica, Alejandra and Gabriela; for your precious friendship, your encouraging words, your love and your wisdom. Thank you for the hours spent listening to my crazy adventures and ideas. You are the most beautiful, brave and strong women I have known.

To Siri Gopal Kaur and Roshi. Your beautiful healing work and wisdom has supported my spiritual journey. Thank you for believing I was worthy of writing this book. I admire your capacity to share your gifts with the world. You are a huge inspiration in my life.

To my two grandfathers, Roberto and Roberto, my grandmother Conchita and my aunt Maria. I feel the love, spiritual support and protection you offer me from wherever you are. I love and miss you.

To my aunt Patricia and uncle Salvador, for offering their home in Belgium, which allowed me the space to write this book. Thank you for your hospitality and generosity.

To Nery and Jose. Thank you for all the support and care you have provided all these years to Andres and I. Jose, your friendship has made a huge impact in Andres' life. Thank you for always respecting our home. You are truly another son to me. Know that your presence brings light to our lives.

To my friend Jim. Thank you for your positive personality and openness to life's teachings, for helping me review this book and for your continuous support through the years. I value our friendship.

To my ex-husband Mark. Thank you for being so involved in Andres' life. For encouraging him to do his best, supporting him and loving him. I appreciate everything you do for him.

To Natasha Pierre-Louis, Peter Jison and Monica Ramirez for their creativity and hard work in designing the book cover. You did an amazing job.

To the CreateSpace team at Amazon.com, for providing an avenue to new and existing writers for self-publishing. To the book editor, thank you for your input and professionalism.

Finally, I thank life, my greatest teacher, and everyone who has crossed my path. You have been a source of inspiration, wisdom, support, and love.

INTRODUCTION

Busy schedules and social demands are keeping us distant from our true essence, our Being. More than ever, noise, clutter, and distractions have become a part of our lives to the point that we may feel uneasiness without them.

At one time or another, we all have experienced pain through the loss of a loved one, frustration with an unexpected outcome, fear at the idea of an unwanted future event, anger or disappointment when someone doesn't act according to our standards, or impatience when we are required to wait for a person to arrive, or a situation to unfold.

Every human has encountered situations that call for introspection. Whether or not we make a decision to stop and take a look inside depends on our state of awareness, our openness, our flexibility, and our willingness to move forward in our spiritual evolution.

Spiritual evolution is a natural process and a process of love. It is a fundamental part of our existence and the manifestation of a larger intelligence where *all* is included and *all* is valid.

This intelligence is beautifully expressed through nature where everything fulfills a function that supports cycles, seasons, and patterns. Every animal, plant, and organism is vital to sustain life.

Each color, shape, and texture is a testimony of a creation that is inclusive, harmonious, abundant, and limitless.

This intelligence, which I also call "life," never chooses, it allows; it never resists, it accepts; it doesn't segregate, it includes. Like nature, all aspects of human reality support a purpose and can be used as a source for transformation. When we use an aspect of our humanity to go within and initiate transformation, I call this "outward meditation." Through our humanity, we access our spirit. Through our spirituality, we can attain consciousness.

Two of the most beautiful gifts we receive throughout our spiritual evolution are the connectedness we all share as Beings and the freedom we own to co-create with life as our timing and readiness permits.

In the course of our existence, we serve many roles and fulfill many purposes, but none of this is possible without everybody's participation. Every role has a function, and every purpose creates a different reality. Situations arrive to grant us the opportunity to grow in spirit by transforming them, but only we hold the freedom to do so, when we are ready. This is the manifestation of awareness.

For a few, awareness arrives as a mystical experience, resulting in a profound realization of Being, breaking all attachments and therefore dissolving ego. For the rest of us, awareness arrives at moments. As we evolve spiritually, what I call our *conscious moments* increase in frequency. However, this evolution implies introspection, kindness to oneself, a profound sense of trust toward the flow of life, and our active participation by initiating action.

In this process of self-awareness, we begin to recognize the relationship between our humanity and our spirituality. We become familiar with our perceptions and habits. At the same time, moments of peace, joy, and clarity arrive with regularity. From this place of recognition, we begin to create balance in every area of our lives. We initiate action, and our intentions manifest. This is spiritual evolution at its best; it is everyone's most beautiful project and purpose. It is realized with the help of everyone and everything. Nothing is misused and nothing is wasted because life is all inclusive, whole, and eternal.

This book introduces spiritual practices and suggestions that can be instrumental in attaining clarity, as you move forward in your spiritual evolution.

The chapters are presented in a sequence I thought would be best for maintaining continuity and flow, but they don't have to be read in order. Each sentence is a proposition based on my observations of my own ways to connect within, my "ego moments" as well as my *conscious moments,* and observations based on personal experiences and the experiences of others, some close to me and some I have never even met but who have profoundly transformed my perceptions.

We are able to access peace, acceptance, and clarity in the midst of any situation. We know how to attract abundance, set intentions, and witness their manifestation. We have only to remember how this is consciousness: the return to the knowledge we have held all along.

There are many spiritual practices we can use to help us arrive at awareness and create a balanced and joyful life experience. I present eight practices that can be followed at any time and anywhere. As mentioned, we travel through life with different timing for transformation, so respect and kindness toward our individual process is important.

This book is a celebration of life. Its content is meant to empower you. It presents ways in which you can use your daily life and the aspects of your humanity to access clarity and transform your existence. Only you can travel this journey, no one can do it for you. Trust that all is a source for transformation. With your actions, create the life you want, and help renew the world around you.

With my deepest gratitude.

PRACTICE 1

SIMPLIFYING YOUR LIFE: ALLOWING SPACE TO MANIFEST

When we live a life of simplicity, we allow the space necessary for life to flow through it. We can see with clarity what really matters.

Space cannot be explained—it can be experienced, or allowed. It is manifested everywhere. It exists in the universe, our planet, our homes, our bodies, our Being, between the notes of a song, between the words of a conversation. Space promotes positive energy whenever we allow it, and through it, we can access clarity, the doorway to self-realization.

The space you occupy: your home

A home is a place through which you can express your personality. Colors on the walls, décor items, and keepsakes communicate your likes and preferences. Besides reflecting your personality, a home reflects your habits and views. The place you inhabit becomes a projection of who you are, internally and externally.

We spend a third of our life in our homes. Currently, the average lifespan of an American is seventy-six years, and that means around twenty-five years are spent inside our living space. As you allow space in your home, there is an opening for nurturing and love, and you begin to find opportunities to practice detachment and express gratitude through your home.

Transforming your life through space

I once heard, "The clutter you have outward is equal to the clutter you have inward." Internal clutter is projected into the external world and affects other areas in life, creating imbalance, promoting negativity, and obstructing space.

Balance, or a lack of it, shows in the way we live. When we experience stability, joy, clarity, and peace within ourselves, the environment we inhabit reflects the same state.

When there is clutter, there is disorder and confusion. Clutter is a distraction and occupies the space we need to acquire clarity. Clutter externalizes in many ways: accumulating unnecessary possessions, excessive time spent in front of computers, the playing of video games, or watching TV, surrounding ourselves with unhealthy people, drama, disorder, constant noise and any form of negativity. We fill our lives with so many distractions that there is little or no space to promote personal growth.

Using our home to become more conscious is one of many ways to reach inward. It is as helpful and life changing as meditation, praying, or yoga. Getting rid of clutter is a form of outward meditation. It promotes beautiful practices such as detachment, cleanliness, and order. We practice detachment in how we learn to be happy and comfortable with just the necessary. Our dependency on material things to feel joy diminishes, and we realize that the more we let go of, the less we need. When there is order, we are communicating that everything has its place and that everything deserves respect for its existence. We value all we have and become more grateful for it.

As we get rid of clutter, we begin to live with simplicity, and this simplicity is reflected in other areas of our life. For example, we travel lighter, we don't consume as much, we become more aware of the value that everything holds, it is easier to detach from material things, and we diminish the use of entertainment media for self-distraction.

Another way to de-clutter, is by getting rid of things that occupy space without serving us in a functional, practical, or positive way.

Anything that is not absolutely necessary, doesn't serve us, or we don't deeply love and care for can be released.

For a lot of people, getting rid of things is extremely hard. If that is the case for you, start by de-cluttering in small quantities. Some clothes that haven't been worn in a while can be donated to charity. Sale unused CDs to a music store, and use the money toward a trip to visit a close friend. We tend to accumulate books and some of them we don't look at, while others have been read already. Keep the books you cherish the most. The ones you won't read again or feel that others will enjoy can be donated to a local library or school.

Every item you get rid of has served its purpose, and now other people can enjoy it. The space that item occupied is necessary for new and fresh energy to enter. Each time you get rid of something, you practice detachment.

You can also de-clutter by minimizing distractions. Music, TV, computers, video games, and other forms of entertainment can be fun, but heavy media use keeps you from spending time in your own company or the company of people you enjoy being with.

When many hours are spent in front of computers or TVs, little or no time is left for self-discovery or introspection. According to the A.C. Nielsen Co., the average American watches more than four hours of TV each day, which adds up to two months per year. This means that in a sixty-five-year life, the average American will have spent a total of nine years in front of the TV. The same company provides facts about online use. Americans spend a staggering 2,621,000 hours online each month. In June 2010, the number of videos streamed passed the ten billion mark, and the average American consumer spent three hours and fifteen minutes streaming online videos during the month.

The entertainment industry's primary function is to keep us needing or wanting what it offers, and most of what it offers doesn't particularly promote self-growth. A lot of media content is charged with ideas or concepts that provoke negative feelings and pollute not only the energy in the environment but, most importantly, the energy we carry within. Distractions take away precious time that could be used for productivity and positivism, service to others, introspection, volunteer work, strengthening our relationships, nurturing our body, enjoying a personal hobby, or taking care of a situation that requires our attention.

Parents have a great opportunity to pass on to their children qualities that promote simplicity. By not accumulating unnecessary things and minimizing the use of entertainment media, we teach them to practice detachment, and we show them how to spend time in their own company without needing entertainment for their enjoyment.

A national survey by the Kaiser Family Foundation presents the dramatic rise on the amount of time that young people spend with entertainment media. [1] "Today, 8-18 year-olds devote an average of 7 hours and 38 minutes (7:38) to using entertainment media across a

23

typical day (more than 53 hours a week). And because they spend so much of that time 'media multitasking' (using more than one medium at a time), they actually manage to pack a total of 10 hours and 45 minutes (10:45) worth of media content into those 71/2 hours." The report was released in January 2010 at a forum in Washington, DC.

Our children are precious, and their development, life habits, and spiritual evolution are shaped by the degree of balance they experience. Starting from an early age, we can help them build a strong foundation by decreasing distracting activities such as media entertainment that cut them off from their awareness and detract from a healthy, balanced life. There are many activities that can empower them and enhance their daily experience in a constructive way. They can enjoy a walk outside with you, learn to cook, paint, read a book, practice a sport, learn to play an instrument, or participate in a volunteer program.

Most of what we pass on to our children is by example. If we try to teach our children values and healthy habits that we don't practice ourselves, we contradict our words with our behaviors. Our words will have little credibility, and our children will be confused. To provoke change in others, we must initiate change in ourselves.

A society based in consumerism teaches us that more is never enough, that bigger is better, and that the more expensive an item is, the greater the owner's status. We have come to believe that owning something made by a specific brand name will make a difference in the way we feel or view ourselves. We all know that the satisfaction we experience when we purchase something is never permanent, and invariably makes us want to obtain more. We live in a society that thrives on instant gratification and have forgotten that joy arrives when we live in peace and gratitude regardless of material belongings, titles, or social class. When we can enjoy material things but can be joyful without them, we have true freedom.

We also have the opportunity to pass to our children the habit of not accumulating toys, by donating every so often a few of their used toys to less fortunate children. Learning to share will strengthen their capacity to be of service and be compassionate to others. They can learn detachment at an early age, experience the joy that comes when they give, and begin to disassociate from status when they employ principles of simplification with our guidance and encouragement.

Our spirit doesn't need anything. True joy comes from the love we can experience toward others, nature, the world, and ourselves. Abundance is not represented by how much we accumulate but in the quality of our existence projected in our living space, our relationships, our jobs, and our daily life.

Creating balance between our humanity and our spirituality may require work but is a vital part of the process as we evolve spiritually. Every day is filled with opportunities to practice detachment. We can simplify our lives by sharing instead of accumulating. We can contribute to good health by living in spaces that communicate order and cleanliness.

Use your home to create a space that reflects the values you want to enhance your life with, and extend the same principal to other areas of your life that may need transformation.

Discovering your home as a source for transformation

Gratitude is the action of honoring life. When we talk about instant gratification, we talk about what gratitude is: a practice that creates immediate transformation and a profound feeling of joy at the same time. I devoted all of Chapter 6 to the practice of gratitude, because it is one of the most empowering and enthusiastic aspects of our spirituality.

We often take for granted the many ways in which a home serves us. Regardless of its size, a home gives us shelter and comfort. It allows us space for gatherings and celebrations; it is a vehicle for expressing creativity and nurturing inspiration. It is also the space where we are able to spend quality time with our loved ones and build memories that last a lifetime.

Basic services like running water and electricity permit us to cook, wash our clothes, or take a hot shower. Such activities may seem simple and unimportant because we are used to them, but because of them we can live in a clean and comfortable environment.

Kitchen appliances are practical, to say the least, allowing us to cut, mix, prepare, bake, wash, and cook with more ease. Our home may provide us with a beautiful view of a garden or a stunning view of a city. Windows allow light to enter every morning, and the roof protects us from the weather. Because of the location, we may have access to beautiful areas where we can enjoy nature at a park, or amenities such as restaurants.

It is common to have unexpected malfunctions in a household. Perhaps a dishwasher breaks hours before a big party. Maybe you are hosting friends from out of town, and the heater stops working, leaving you with no hot water, or a leak produces a flood and damages the carpet you just installed. These situations can be frustrating, but they are also perfect situations for self-improvement. As it helps you move from frustration to patience, from lack of control to acceptance—your house can be a great vehicle for transformation. There are many reasons and endless opportunities to be grateful for the space you inhabit and all that comes with it.

We have all heard the saying, "We don't know what we have until it is gone." Similarly, when something in the house stops working, it gives us the opportunity to value it for all the benefits that it provides when it works. Gratitude attracts abundance and produces joy, it promotes positive energy whenever we express it, and it's free. If a home is a reflection of who we are, it is important to treat everything in it with the same respect and care we treat ourselves. This is deeply linked to attracting abundance. We cannot expect to have more if we don't respect and feel grateful for what we have in the present moment.

Sharing space with others

We all share or have shared living space with others. Accommodating everyone's needs in the household requires flexibility and the active participation of everybody sharing the space.

Invariably things wear out or need maintenance. Numerous chores must be taken care of to maintain order, cleanliness, and functionality in the space we occupy, and accomplishing them requires consistency and organization.

The distribution of chores among everyone who shares space in the household is vital to promote an environment of teamwork and purpose. In this case, the purpose is to create an atmosphere that reflects family values, where harmony and positive energy are the norm, where each member has opportunities for self-expression and self-nurturing, and where differences are respected.

Coach Dean Smith said to Michael Jordan in his freshman year at UNC, "Michael, if you can't pass, you can't play." If each member of a family or household wants to enjoy the benefits that a home offers, he must also contribute to its care and maintenance. If only one person carries the responsibilities in the household, the other members don't experience the rewards and lessons of participation, teamwork, and service.

Teamwork can be challenging but is an action that brings everyone together. It raises awareness as participants realize the unlimited ways in which they can promote values in the home, as well as the importance of caring and being grateful for what they have.

"Teamwork" exercise

To create an atmosphere of teamwork in your household, the following four steps are important.

1. Set a common purpose.

Explain to the members of your household all the benefits of living in a space that reflects stability. Ask the members what they like about their house and why. Talk about the importance of working as a team and its rewards. Set a purpose that reflects your values as a family. Your purpose must be clear and must communicate the type of environment you want to live in.

Make your family purpose short and clear. Print it on a piece of paper, and place it in each room and in a common gathering place such as the kitchen. Here is an example:

"Our family, (Family Name), wants to live in an environment where mutual respect, caring for what we have, and communication are the norm. Everyone is to respect the space he has been assigned. Every member of the household commits to treating everything in the house with care and respect and assumes the responsibility for carrying out his chores. We all commit to use communication in a peaceful way when we express disagreement or dissatisfaction."

2. Assign age-appropriate chores.

Not every member of a household is the same age and has the same capabilities, so it is important to assign chores accordingly. If necessary, set expectations on the time and/or day for completion.

Example:

Paul (ten years old)

Every day

Bedroom: Will make his bed in the morning, will place his dirty clothes in the hamper in the bathroom, and put away his toys before he goes to sleep.

A common area: Will make the lemonade at supper time.

Once a week

He will sweep the entrance of the house and the patio every Saturday.

Sofia (fourteen years old)

Every day

Bedroom: Will make her bed in the morning and will keep her room orderly and clean by putting items in their place. – (You can add a note that reads, "The floor is not their place.")

A common area: She will set the table at supper time and will help out with cooking.

Once a week

Every Saturday, she will wash, fold, and put away her clothes, will vacuum her bedroom and her brother's bedroom. Every other weekend, she will mow the lawn.

You can also set general household chores such as, "Everyone is to put their dishes in the dishwasher after each meal."

3. Commitment and responsibility.

Each member of the family is to write a "commitment statement" that communicates to himself and the others what he has agreed to do. Commitment builds trust and character among team members. Each member of the family can write his statement on a piece of paper as a testimony of his commitment allowing him to cultivate ownership.

Example:

"I, Michael, commit to _____. I will make my best effort to complete the chores I have agreed to do and will show a positive attitude as I complete them."

4. Assign a mentor.

Each member of the family should be assigned a mentor. Through his support, the mentor will encourage the other person to accomplish her chores, and will point out with kindness when the person is lacking enthusiasm or is not taking responsibility for her part. The mentor is to remind the person how and why is important to keep harmony in the household.

Explain the role of the mentor and how important it is to empower others by example. A mentor must follow through with his actions before asking others to do the same. You can assign a mentor or do a raffle and switch mentors periodically. This will give the mentor a sense of responsibility as well as the opportunity to empower another person.

Change doesn't occur overnight—it takes everyone's willingness and participation to make it happen. If cooperation and teamwork are challenges in your household, start with yourself. Positive action can be contagious, and when done without expecting anything in return, it allows space for others to act in the same way.

A greener space

The space we inhabit can contribute to the well-being of our planet. According to the Environmental Protection Agency, the average American produces about 4.4 pounds of garbage a day, or a total of 1,600 pounds a year. Reducing garbage production, recycling, using eco-friendly materials, reducing consumption of electricity and water, and buying only what we need are a few of the many ways that can create a greener space and therefore a greener world.

Spiritual growth is expressed in our capacity to be compassionate and empathetic toward others. We inhabit this planet with others and are responsible for its care, individually and collectively. We can be conscious supporters to the stability of our environment by taking care of the space each of us occupies, and this action alone will make a difference in the type of world we inhabit.

We have become a "disposable" society where we purchase and item and easily dispose it as soon as some new, faster or more expensive model comes out. Companies have found creative ways to make us feel "out of style" if we don't own the latest model of their products.

Excessive consumerism and rapid disposal doesn't only damage the environment by contributing to pollution, but it can also keep us trapped in a mindset that seeks enjoyment only on form and forgets how rewarding a life of simplicity can be. This idea is beautifully described by Donald Horban: "We don't need to increase our goods nearly as much as we need to scale down our wants. Not wanting something is as good as possessing it."

Living a life of simplicity is a decision and a practice that enhances our lives not with material things but with values. When we allow space to manifest, life can flow through it. Life corresponds by providing situations and people that help us move forward in our spiritual evolution. We move with life, and life moves through us in ways that are gracious, effortless, and harmonious.

Simplify your life by doing less, having less and buying less. A schedule packed with activities, a household filled with clutter, and a mind occupied with distractions obstructs the space needed to access clarity. Leonardo da Vinci said, "Simplicity is the ultimate sophistication."

Suggestions

Live in simplicity by getting rid of clutter in your home.

De-cluttering the house and organizing the space you share can be a fun activity for the whole family. Do one room every weekend, or assign one room to each family member. Separate useful items from those that are not necessary and donate them to non-profit organizations or have a yard sale. The gains from the yard sale can be put toward a trip you have wanted to do for a long time, a hobby you want to take on, or deposited in a savings account.

Keep your home clean and in order.

Cleanliness and order promote the flow of positive energy and good health. Open the windows, and let the air and light enter the house. Keep cabinets and drawers organized and clean. Tools such as Feng Shui and Vatsu Shastra—both ancient sciences that teach how to balance the energies in any space, can be used to enhance your well-being in the way you place furniture or items in your household.

Create a special place in your home for self-expression and nurturing.

Choose a place in your home where you can do activities that nurture you, activities that you enjoy and love. This can be an area for reading, meditation, yoga, playing an instrument, or painting. Have fun with it. This is an area meant for you to express who you are and your intentions. Other members of your family or household may do the same if they choose to.

Allow no negativity in your space.

Invite to your home people who promote the beliefs and values you live by. Diminish your distractions by spending less time with entertainment media and more time in your own company or the company of those you love. When you use entertainment media, try to look for material that promotes your values, for example: documentaries, inspiring biographies or shows about nature.

Practice 2

The Gift of Silence: Clarity Arrives

Clarity manifests in that place where no distractions exist, where silence is welcomed and cherished for the gift that it is.

Silence is a portal through which we access clarity. Clarity allows us to make more conscious decisions, and it helps us navigate through life without fear. When we are clear, our intuition awakens, and we are able to listen and trust it every time we need to make a decision. When our choices come from a place of clarity, the outcome is always a peaceful one, whatever it may be. When we make decisions from a place of confusion, the result may be charged with suffering, deception, frustration, anger, or more confusion.

Learning to appreciate, seek, and love silence is a process. For many of us, it is a foreign concept and not an easy practice, especially if we are talkative, share our opinions with others often, or seek attention or approval by using words.

Music lovers may find the idea of loving silence unimaginable. With CD and MP3 players, radios and smart phones, music or any type of audio are available to us 24/7. A large number of people listen to something in their car, their house, their office, while they exercise, and even in the shower.

Music is one of humanity's most beautiful expressions. It is an art form and a source for inspiration and joy, but like anything, when listened to in excess, it leaves little to no space for self-introspection. We cannot hear our interior voice because we are too busy hearing something else. We don't realize that we are blocking one of the greatest paths to learning about ourselves and accessing clarity within.

A lot of us feel uncomfortable, even terrorized, by the idea of practicing silence. We don't know what to do in our own company without distractions. We are afraid to be with our thoughts, feelings, or fears, so we look for ways to block them. Self-realization starts from a place of clarity, and silence is a powerful and effective practice to help us arrive at this place with ease. A few minutes of silence everyday are sufficient for transformation to flourish, and like anything done with consistency, the more we do it, the more it becomes an essential part of our existence.

Despite all the exposure and the opportunities I had throughout my life to use silence as a portal for introspection, I showed little appreciation toward its benefits, and certainly perceived it more as an obstacle, than a blessing.

As time passed, I began to notice that people who talked constantly and were opinionated bothered me. I couldn't figure out why until I became aware that those people were a reflection of the traits I didn't like about myself. I realized that during conversations it was hard for me to know when or how to stop talking. I wanted to impose my opinion and I had a tough time listening to others. Something in me wanted to change that, but I didn't know how, or where to begin.

Through a friend, I heard of a center in New York where retreats of many types were offered. In their catalog, I found a retreat that seemed interesting, and decided to attend. Among other activities, the center offered meditation sessions as well as Tai Chi and yoga classes every day. Nature, the gardens, and areas for meditation invited me to practice silence. Up in the mountains, cell phone reception wasn't accessible so phone calls weren't an option. I didn't have a computer with me. For a week, it seemed as if I was living on another planet where the inhabitants consumed organic food, walked in silence, practiced yoga, and did meditation—a planet where people were inspired and looked joyful. I took walks in silence and did the meditations. I took the yoga classes and did the chanting. I made an effort to listen, to be more present, to give others the space to talk and share who they were. I began to realize that, in doing these new tasks, I was becoming more patient with myself, less critical of others, and more clear about the type of life I wanted to live and the choices I needed to make to get there. Silence was helping me to become more aware of others and of myself as well.

After the retreat, we entered Manhattan during rush hour on a Friday afternoon. The contrast between the peaceful atmosphere at the retreat and the chaos of the city hit me abruptly. I felt as if I was again on another planet. I started paying attention to the noise, the sirens, and drivers beeping cars horns. There were rivers of people passing by, everyone trying so desperately to get somewhere, and most looked tired, angry or stressed-out. The reality I had returned to seemed so foreign to me.

I felt panic and wanted to return to the peacefulness I had just discovered. "Maybe I can get a job at the retreat house," I thought. I wanted to experience feelings of peace, joy, detachment, and self-love in my everyday life.

I began to see my reality as an obstacle because it didn't resemble in many ways what I had experienced at the retreat. I started questioning how I could create a life of balance. How could I practice silence in a place where noise was the norm? How could I feel inspired in spite of the routine? How could I use my life situations to feel at peace, to be more compassionate, to be more conscious?

The answer came. A voice inside of me said, "Start practicing whenever you can and wherever you are, the values that you want to live your life by."

My first attempt to create a more conscious and balanced life was to spend five days in complete silence: no talking, no TV, no listening to the radio or music, no use of electronics, no phone calls. Silence was to become my loyal companion.

My only way of communication was through writing and only if absolutely necessary. At work, I explained to my boss what I was trying to do. Luckily he was understanding and agreed to let me take on this crazy idea if I communicated work-related issues by email. A few days before I began "fasting" (using no words), I told my closest family members and friends what I was doing so they wouldn't call or visit.

For the most part, everyone was supportive—although a few thought I was completely out of my mind and no one understood why I was doing it. I knew this endeavor wasn't going to hurt me and could definitely help me. I was curious and excited. I wanted to learn more about myself and wondered whether or not I would be able to do such a thing. I had no idea if or how I was going to survive five days with no entertainment, no visitors, no phone calls, reading or talking. Little did I know that I was about to go through a life-changing experience.

I was in what it felt like a marathon of silence. It made me think of those times when I was told not to do something, and the moment I was deprived of it, I craved it even more. Are you kidding me? I wanted to talk more than ever before and started thinking that what I had set out to do was an impossible task.

At first, it was extremely challenging, especially at work. I wanted to give my opinions, and it took a lot out of me to not do so. As the days went by, being in silence became easier and almost enjoyable. At home, there wasn't background music. Simple activities like folding clothes, cutting vegetables, or sweeping became a way of meditating, a reason for introspection. There were no conversations on the phone, no interruptions, nothing to entertain me, and nothing to distract me from my own realization. I started paying more attention to my actions and feelings. I realized that by sitting and doing nothing, I was practicing patience. I became more present and began to enjoy my own company.

Not speaking showed me how to be more appreciative of times that I am able to communicate with others. I was deprived of my daily "I love you" to my son or the "good morning" to my coworkers, or the excitement that comes when good news are shared with a friend or a loved one. It made me realize that I took the gift of words for granted. At the same time, it taught me to choose words with more care and not underestimate their power. Silence taught me to listen to others and learn from them. Silence taught me that I don't need entertainment in any of its forms to have fun and that the sound of the rain is as amazing as any of my favorite songs.

A companion had suddenly surfaced. This companion didn't judge, question, or attack me. This companion allowed me to be; it was kind, loving, and accepting. It had always been there and it would never leave. I just needed to discover it, and through it, discover me.

Silence is now a precious gift to me, as vital as breathing. It is always accessible. I just have to open the door to it, and it kindly enters to show me more of all that I hold within.

I often spend long periods of time in silence, it allows me to get centered, to find clarity when I need answers to a situation, or simply to be in my own company. My son and I have what we call "Silence Day." On our day of silence, we speak—but no music, radio, TV, computers, videogames, or phone calls are welcomed. We spend quality time with each other and do activities that inspire us or ignite feelings of enthusiasm and joy. We take walks or go for a swim, cook together, read a book, or work on a fun project.

Silence is free and always accessible. It allows for many gifts, the most precious ones being introspection and clarity.

Listening and outward meditation

The main purpose of meditation as a practice is to experience a state of complete peace and awareness of oneself. There are several different types of meditation techniques to help us attain this state, and many of them use silence as a portal.

Day-to-day conversations are another aspect of our humanity through which we can practice outward meditation. Listening implies undivided attention and presence. During a conversation, active listening is a form of meditation through which we give the other person space to share his feelings and points of view. When we listen instead of talk, we have the opportunity to learn from others. Many times, what people really want is for another person to listen. Our capacity to listen is a reflection of our capacity to be compassionate and empathetic toward another.

By practicing active listening during conversations, we can reach within and raise our level of awareness. Listening without interrupting is an act of selflessness and consideration; it invites us to detach from our need to express an opinion. Listening with no judgment implies putting aside the ego and allowing the speaker the freedom to fully express who he is. We practice openness, acceptance and respect. A beautiful gift is given to another when we listen from a place of respect and appreciation of individuality.

When we talk, we are not only talking to the other person, we are also talking to ourselves. From there, we can practice introspection by paying attention to our affirmations, positions, perceptions, and judgments. Conversations give us the opportunity to listen, express, and learn from ourselves and others.

Silence and your intuition

Distractions block the space necessary for awareness to surface. When silence enters this space, there is room for introspection.

Things are put into perspective, and you are able to recognize the signs and messages that are important for your growth. Your intuition becomes more acute.

Messages intended for spiritual evolution come from everywhere—all the time. Have you ever watched a movie that triggers a thought or a feeling related to an important situation in your life? Have you listened to a song whose lyrics exactly describe something you are experiencing at the moment? Have you ever gone to a bookstore and picked a book that got your attention, read it, and found that it served as a source for awakening? How many times have you heard someone say something that questions a point of view or found inspiration in someone's actions? Nothing happens by mistake.

We are all connected, and we are all here to heal ourselves and others. Collectively, we help each other evolve spiritually. When you listen, you are aware and ready to receive the messages that are necessary to help you make decisions or change negative patterns. If silence isn't present in your life, you may not recognize the messages. You may get confused by the noise and activity of daily distractions and miss information necessary to take a specific action.

The more silence there is outward, the more clarity there is inward. The space for self-observation is allowed, and self-observation brings clarity. It doesn't matter what situation you encounter—if there is clarity, there is trust and flexibility.

Silence and breathing

Breathing is our most primal activity, one that affects us in all levels. Healthy breathing patterns can improve your energy level and your health. The increased oxygenation creates a balance in your nervous system reducing fatigue and stress, two of the main causes of illnesses such as depression, diabetes, heart conditions, and cancer.

Known as *prana, qui, pneuma,* or *ki,* among other terms, the breath has been used for centuries by many cultures as a portal to reach within and increase spiritual awareness.

Silence is vital in becoming more in tune with your breathing. To improve your breathing pattern, it is necessary to pay attention to the breath itself and also to the silence in between each breath. This is the action of conscious breathing. It improves your health and aids you in creating a state of peace.

Silence is an invitation to intimacy where introspection takes place. It facilitates awareness and balance, and it should never be forced but welcomed. Through it, we access our inner voice, the voice of pure wisdom that allows us to navigate through life with clarity. Silence is a doorway to presence; it is a healer, a teacher, and a true gift.

Suggestions

Practice silence on a daily basis.

A week of silence is healing and helpful but not imperative to receive benefits. A few minutes of silence per day are sufficient to ignite transformation. Start with half an hour a day of complete silence (no talking, if you choose). As you feel more comfortable, add time in thirty-minute increments until you are able to be in silence for longer periods.

Experience the benefits of silence as a family.

Silence is a beautiful practice that the whole family can benefit from. Start by introducing silence once a week: no entertainment media for an hour, including TV, computers, video games, radio, and music. Add time until you are able to spend at least one hour per day together, as a family, without noise.

Use silence for introspection.

During conversations, practice active listening by paying attention to the speaker. Make an effort to listen more and talk less. When you talk, become aware of your words, and try to pinpoint your affirmations, views, and judgments. Try asking yourself questions such as these: How would a person, who is at peace, participate in this conversation? How would a loving and kind person answer this question? What type of comment would a person, who wants to live in balance, make? If possible, start a "conversation journal," and write your observations. This will help you become more attentive and considerate toward others and less engaged on your position during conversations.

Practice conscious breathing.

Breathe slowly and deeply and wait a few seconds between each breath. Pay attention to the sound of every inhalation and exhalation, as well as the silence between breaths.

PRACTICE 3

SELF-OBSERVATION: A STATE OF BALANCE

Observation, you allow me to see with clarity "All" that I am.

To live in a state of balance, we must pay close attention to every aspect of our Being. Body, mind, and spirit are interconnected—each supports the other and each constantly communicates to us where we are in our spiritual evolution.

Self-observation allows us to see with clarity all we are. From there, we decide how and when we want to initiate change toward a better and more balanced life.

Life is experienced individually. Each person goes through it in a unique way, but our common denominator is our spirit. Spirit (soul or consciousness) moves through energy and communicates through expressions of love, kindness, compassion, joy, gratitude, and peace. Its voice is our intuition, our teacher, our guide. This voice speaks *only* the language of love and kindness. It never imposes or judges, and it *always* supports our well-being.

Self-observation is very much like dating yourself. When you date someone, you invest time and energy into that person. You cannot wait to see him, you want to look your best, and you want to know everything you can about him. Time and energy allow you to know each other deeply, and you begin to fall in love. From that place of love, you accept each other as you both are.

In the same way, time, energy, care, and love invested toward self-awareness result in clarity, and you begin to fall in love with all of your Being. As a result of self-realization, you feel comfortable in your own company, and your perception of the world changes because change is occurring inside of you.

Lack of change reinforces old patterns that keep you stuck in unfulfilled expectations, choices based on confusion, negative feelings, and a constant state of wanting and needing.

Introspection is most beneficial if done from a place of silence and solitude. Silence is necessary to hear your inner voice, your intuition. We have talked about the many benefits that silence provides—solitude grants the space for awakening to manifest inward and enables you to feel joyful in your own company.

Experiencing solitude

There is a difference between being alone and feeling lonely and experiencing solitude. Being alone is a physical state where no one is around you. Feeling lonely is an emotional state. You can be surrounded by people and still feel lonely. Loneliness is underlined by feelings of emptiness, sadness, anxiety, and often, fear. When you feel lonely, you lack trust in your inner strength and are unable to find comfort and joy in your own company. Experiencing solitude is a spiritual gift; you establish a deep connection within yourself and, from there, recognize the unconditional love and support that life offers you.

Solitude facilitates the space to identify thought as well as behavior patterns, likes and dislikes, values, dreams and goals. Through solitude, you can access a purpose and discover the actions needed to take in order to fulfill it. You can acknowledge your boundaries and experience acceptance when you face your limitations.

Life moves in perfect balance and your Being is a mirror image of that perfection. The imbalance you experience in life has nothing to do with life itself; it is the result of accumulated emotions, attachments, and unhealthy patterns that create layers of negativity and impede you from connecting deeply with that perfection.

Removing these layers requires self-observation and actively initiating your transformation.

As you practice self-observation and arrive at a place of self-realization, you take ownership of your existence and everything that comes with it. You no longer expect others to take responsibility for your choices or actions. Your joy and fulfillment are no longer dependent on others.

The damaging effects of guilt

Guilt is one of the most damaging emotions you can experience. Attached to belief systems imprinted in your subconscious, guilt keeps you in a state of regret. Thoughts associated with guilt sabotage your spiritual evolution by weakening your Being with negativity. Self-attacks and self-blame go hand in hand with inferiority, anger, culpability, inadequacy, and feeling flawed.

Guilt is the result of decisions made and actions taken in the past. You cannot bring back the past. Transformation can occur only in the present. If there is an action in your past that you would like to have done differently, use your present situations to create change. Sooner or later, life will bring another opportunity for you to initiate transformation. When this happens, awareness is vital to taking actions that promote a positive outcome.

Practicing self-observation will create space to find the lessons behind each situation that arrives. When you welcome these lessons and grow from them, you take responsibility for your Being.

Every situation arrives with the purpose to show you something, to guide you and to allow for awareness to manifest. Life is wisdom, and it always presents opportunities for growth to happen, but personal growth is a decision born out of clarity. It cannot be forced. Life invites you over and over to create transformation, and it is up to you to accept the invitation.

Taking responsibility for your actions must be done from a place of kindness, from where you look at your past as a guide and teacher, not as a judge. When you use kindness instead of guilt, you heal yourself and others. Along with acceptance and love, kindness is an attribute of compassion, so think of it as a bonus. Every time you look at any situation or person from a place of kindness, you practice compassion. Where there is kindness, guilt cannot exist.

Kindness toward oneself

The first time I heard someone say "be kind to yourself," it sounded like a foreign concept. I knew how to be kind to others, but it was difficult to find ways to be kind to myself.

To promote kindness toward yourself, become aware of how you may be promoting the opposite behavior, and initiate transformation. When unkindness is expressed with regularity, it becomes a habit and can be hard to identify. Unkind actions damage your body, mind and spirit, slowing your personal growth.

Unkindness is often expressed by not paying attention to our needs, or lack of self-nurturing.

Below are some examples of ways in which we can nurture our body, mind and spirit.

Maintain a healthy diet.

A healthy diet provides you with protein, minerals, vitamins, and nutrients. It lowers your risk of illnesses, improves your immune system, keeps your cholesterol under control, boosts your energy, and improves your bodily functions. Try to eat organic vegetables, fruits, nuts, protein, and whole grains. Organic farms maintain the integrity of their products by not using pesticides, preservatives, irradiation or artificial ingredients.

Keep your body hydrated.

Drink plenty of water. Water helps your body digest food better and purifies it by flushing out toxins. By keeping your body hydrated, you decrease your risk of heart attacks and cancer, increase your energy, and contribute to healthier skin.

Exercise.

Consistent exercise nurtures your organs, muscles, bones, and every cell. It improves flexibility and balance. It also helps you prevent obesity and subsequent illnesses like heart attacks, diabetes, and stroke.

Practice meditation, yoga or prayer.

Any form of spiritual practice decreases stress by increasing feelings of gratitude, forgiveness, self-love, joy, and peace. These feelings promote the free flow of energy inside your body, improving your health, mind, and general well-being.

Allow your body to rest.

Make an effort to get enough sleep. Studies indicate that when you don't get enough sleep, you increase the risk for illnesses such as cancer, diabetes, obesity, and heart disease. Lack of sleep also contributes to low performance during the day and more serious situations as car accidents or accidents using machinery.

Laugh often.

Many studies have been made that support the benefits of laughter. It strengthens the immune system, decreases pain, raises energy levels, and most importantly, can help release stress.

Have a positive attitude.

A positive attitude improves your relationships, your work and home environments, and your overall well-being. A positive attitude is a reflection of openness, flexibility, and gratitude. When you have a positive attitude, life flows through you with ease, and is viewed as a gift, regardless of the situation.

No one but you is responsible for providing balance in your life. No one but you experiences the benefits of kindness to oneself or the consequences of self-mistreatment. When you treat your Being with kindness, you show how much you value all you are and send life the message, "I love you, I respect you, I am grateful for you."

Unkind thoughts

Another common expression of unkindness toward oneself is negative thoughts. Thoughts such as "I always make the same mistake," "I am really stupid," "with my bad luck," "I cannot believe I did that," and "my problem is" are charged with negativity affecting your health and weakening your spirit.

When you allow your thoughts to promote negativity, you block spiritual evolution from manifesting. Because negativity limits you, it bounds you to view yourself from only one point of view:

insufficiency. You are saying "I am not good enough, I am not beautiful enough, I am not intelligent enough," and so on.

Positivism is expansive and affirming. It allows you openness and the freedom to explore different possibilities. Rather than binding you to a low view of yourself, it empowers you.

Become more aware of your thoughts, and begin identifying the emotions that are generated by them. Thoughts that provoke feelings of sadness, inadequacy, fear, guilt or anger are destructive and self-denying. Thoughts that provoke feelings of kindness, compassion, peace, joy and love are empowering.

Observe your thoughts

Your perception of life influences your thoughts. When thoughts are repetitive, a root system begins to grow in your subconscious. It creates thought patterns, which become your belief system.

Thought patterns consist of affirmations, judgments, comparisons, attacks, or reminders that generate either positive or negative emotions. These have the power to alter your body chemistry and can be an obstacle or support throughout your spiritual evolution.

Negative thought patterns are damaging. The emotions they generate can cause stress, suffering, and fear. But thinking can also be an entryway to peace and freedom, if we learn to transform negative thought patterns into positive ones.

By observing your thoughts, you can identify the emotions generated by them—this is clarity. From a place of clarity, you are able to transform any negative thought and its emotions into those that empower you.

We are not trying to observe every single thought that arrives. Thoughts that promote positive feelings are already serving life's most beautiful purpose: your spiritual awakening. The intention is to observe only those thoughts that generate negative feelings and have become obstacles to your personal growth.

Five steps to observing and transforming your thoughts

Step 1: Welcome the thought.

When a thought that generates a negative feeling arrives, welcome it as your guide. Pushing it away will block awareness. For a few seconds, hold it, and be aware of its presence.

Step 2: Identify the emotions and the reasons generated by the thought.

Identify the emotions generated when the thought arrives. It may be a predominant emotion or a combination of different ones. Next, identify the reason behind the emotions: why do you feel that way?

Step 3: Take ownership of your emotions.

Once you have identified the emotions generated by the thought, own them. Blaming an external source for your feelings is unproductive; you cannot change a situation or a person, you can only ignite change in yourself. Instead concentrate on your feelings. Owning your feelings and taking responsibility for them allows you to change unhealthy thought patterns.

Step 4: Transform the thought.

Transform the thought by creating a "new thought" that is the opposite of the thought you want to transform. The new thought must generate positive emotions that empower you and contribute to your spiritual evolution.

Step 5: Repeat the "new thought."

Thought patterns are created through repetition; when a negative thought reappears, repeat the new thought several times. Eventually it will replace the old thought with the new, creating healthier thought patterns.

Example:

Step 1: Welcome the thought.

For a few seconds, breathe slowly and deeply while you hold the thought.

Thought: "My sister is so ungrateful. She never calls."

Step 2: Identify the emotions and the reasons generated by the thought.

As you identify each emotion, ask yourself why you feel that way.

"I am angry because she doesn't care about me. She always has better things to do than call me (anger)."

"I am disappointed because I am the one who always calls her (disappointment)."

Step 3: Take ownership of your emotions.

Own your emotions by writing down, before the reason, the words "I feel."

"Anger: I feel that she doesn't care about me. I feel that she has better things to do than call."

"Disappointment: I feel that I am the one who always calls."

Step 4: Transform the thought.

Transform the thought by creating a new thought that promotes positive feelings.

New thought: "I love my sister and I am grateful for her. I will call her often to show her how much I care about her."

Step 5: Repeat the new thought.

Every time the old thought "my sister is so ungrateful, she never calls" arrives, repeat, "I love my sister and I am grateful for her. I will call her often to show her how much I care."

A thought is just that: a thought. It arrives to help you gain awareness. The power to create suffering or peace lies in your capacity to transform it.

Transformation leads to well-being, peace, joy, kindness, balance, and clarity, turning your life into a journey of self-love and self-realization. It cannot occur without your active participation; your actions must support and correspond to the values you wish to cultivate.

Collective participation

Life situations guide you throughout your spiritual evolution by showing you which aspects of your life need improvement, adjustment, or transformation. In the same way, the lives of others hold teachings that can be instrumental in increasing your personal awareness. In some cases, you are able to recognize in others habits and values you would like to apply in your daily life or perhaps already practice. In other cases, a person might serve as a reflection of a trait within you that is calling for transformation. Some people show up in your life momentarily, sharing messages or showing you with their actions ways in which awakening can take place in you. Others stay in your life for longer periods, giving you the opportunity, over and over, to obtain awareness through them.

You participate in raising the world's collective awareness through your most powerful contribution: your actions. Self-awareness is a gift from each individual, and the action that results from awareness is a gift to the world.

World transformation starts with self-transformation. You cannot expect the world around you to change if you don't take responsibility for your own transformation. Compassion and love for others starts with self-love and self-kindness. Your actions have a powerful effect on those you share your life with and, subsequently, the world. Your actions shape the world outside you.

Transformation takes place one small step at a time. You honor your life every time you act with kindness toward yourself or another Being. You respect your life every time you are respectful of the individuality of others. You love yourself every time you love without conditions. You experience joy every time you are grateful. You are compassionate when you understand the origin of your own suffering, and therefore the suffering of others. You can be at peace with the world when you are at peace with yourself.

Self-awareness encourages you to push forward. It empowers you to initiate change and inspires you to create and attract new beginnings. Situations always arrive with perfect timing—self-awareness allows you to recognize the lessons behind them and empowers you to transform them, creating a life based on peace. The Dalai Lama XIV said, "It is under the greatest adversity that there exists the greatest potential for doing good, both for oneself and others."

Make self-observation a daily practice. Observe your reactions in situations where you experience suffering, anger, or frustration. Observe your thoughts when you meet someone, your expectations in your relationships, and your feelings when you are alone. The more you practice self-observation, the clearer you become about what moves you, challenges you, changes your mood, or disturbs you.

When decisions are made from a place of clarity, life becomes a journey where people and situations are never seen as obstacles but as guides. Clarity brings the necessary tools to transform negative thought patterns and behavior into those that promote positive feelings. As you show profound love toward others by giving them time and space, do the same for yourself, and experience all the benefits and rewards that come with knowing yourself.

The exercise below helps you to gain clarity through self-observation. Clarity will aid you in creating balance in every aspect of your life.

Make a list of the areas you want to become clearer on or improve (spirituality, health/physical, relationships, professional, financial, etc.).

When doing the exercise, be patient and kind to yourself. I recommend that you to do one area per week to give yourself the space and time necessary for introspection. Trying to accomplish too much at once can leave you feeling overwhelmed and discouraged.

This is your journey. Make the most of these exercises, be honest when writing your answers, and most importantly, have fun with it.

"Clarity" exercise

Area of my life: _____ .

Example: Finance

At the moment, I am/feel: _____ .

(Write a statement that describes your current situation or feelings in that area).

Example: I am in debt. I owe $4,000 on my credit cards.

I would like to: _____ .

(Write a statement that describes what you would like to accomplish or change in the current situation).

Example: I would like to pay off my credit card debt.

My beliefs in this area are (my core values):

I believe that: _____ .

(Write beliefs or perceptions you have in that area).

Example:

I believe that money doesn't grow on trees.

I believe that people with money are not spiritual.

I believe that credit card companies are unfair.

My habits around this area are:

*I have the habit of:*_____.

(Write your habits or behavior patterns around that area).

Example:

I have the habit of going out to eat four days a week.

I have the habit of spending money on things I don't really need.

I have the habit of being disorganized with my finances and don't keep track of my expenses.

*What are my talents?*_____.

(Write your talents, what you are good at).

Example: I am good at math.

Transform your beliefs by writing a positive affirmation:
_____.

(To begin transformation, change your thought patterns into affirmations that describe something positive, constructive, optimistic, or encouraging).

Example:

Transformed beliefs:

Money is represented everywhere. Money exists in abundance.

Money is a great tool that can be used in many ways to create positive outcomes, such as donations, saving for retirement, helping a friend in need, starting a business that will create jobs for others.

There are many people who have a lot of money and are spiritual.

How can I use my talents to create transformation?

_____°

(Write how your talents can be of help in creating transformation).

With my ability to do math, I will create a budget to help me be more organized with my finances.

What actions can I take to transform my habits and behavior?

(Write actions that will transform negative behavior patterns into ones that support your growth. Your plan of action must be realistic to work for you).

Example:

I will go out to eat only two days a week instead of four days. The money I save will be used to pay off my credit cards.

Before I buy something I want, I will consider whether or not I need it. If not, I will not buy it and will use that money to pay off my debt.

Suggestions

Keep a journal of your self-observations.

Write in a journal anything new you observe about yourself; perhaps a reaction you were not expecting, or an action that promoted self-kindness; or maybe your feelings, thoughts and habits about a person that represents a challenge to you.

Spend time in solitude.

Do something in your own company as often as possible. Go to the movies alone, eat at a restaurant by yourself, read a book in solitude, or simply, go outside and do nothing as you observe nature.

Do acts of kindness for yourself.

Treat yourself with a delicious meal you love, take a walk outside, do an activity you enjoy, go to the gym, or take a nap in the middle of the day.

Write down positive affirmations.

Think positive thoughts about your life, your body, personality, spirituality, relationships, and so on. Write these thoughts on index cards and place the cards in your bedroom, house, or office space. Examples might be "I love the opportunity to see my children grow everyday" or "I am grateful to feel so close to my sister" or "I love the color of my eyes."

PRACTICE 4

SETTING BOUNDARIES: PROMOTE SELF-RESPECT

Honor who you are by expressing your boundaries

with love and kindness.

Let me use dancing as a metaphor to illustrate the action of setting boundaries and how they relate to your spiritual evolution. In a dance, you move to the sound of music, and you have your own rhythm and particular moves that are distinctive for you. You probably enjoy some types of music more than others. There may be times that you prefer to watch or listen instead of dancing to the music.

From a spiritual perspective, your moves are your actions. The music represents life situations, and the rhythm to which you dance is your timing and readiness. Situations arrive that require your immediate and imperative participation, and other situations give you the opportunity to decide whether or not you want to participate, as well as when and how you want to do so. This decision is deeply connected to your state of awareness, and the "how" and "when" are based on those boundaries you set for yourself.

Boundaries are set according to three factors: willingness, availability, and readiness. On some occasions, you are willing to do something but are unable to do so. In other occasions, you simply don't feel like participating. And in certain situations, you may be willing and available to participate, but not ready.

People you know might ask for your participation, input, assistance, or support. The willingness to give or be of service to others must be accompanied by one or all of these values: enthusiasm, appreciation, and volunteerism. If you don't feel enthusiastic about doing something, you don't appreciate the cause or the person you are doing it for, or if you feel forced to do something, it is best to not participate.

Setting boundaries implies not only knowing where you stand but also communicating (from a place of love and kindness) your disposition to those involved. Setting boundaries and communicating them with kindness is an expression of self-respect.

Saying "yes" when you are unwilling to participate, or participating out of pressure, creates anger. Accumulated anger results in resentment or related feelings such as annoyance, bitterness, cynicism, or indignation. It is easier to blame others for these feelings, but it is no one's responsibility to make decisions for you. Resentment is directed toward yourself when boundaries are not honored. Sooner or later, resentment will reappear when similar decisions need to be made again. If the situation permits—meaning that your participation is not imperative—honor your boundaries.

Expressing unwillingness or disagreement is often associated with selfishness. There is nothing wrong with setting boundaries and honoring who you are. Honor, respect, and genuineness are fundamental values of sincerity. When boundaries are expressed from a place of sincerity, you support your integrity.

You might not feel comfortable setting boundaries or expressing disagreement because you fear hurting someone or being rejected by someone. When a decision is made from a place of clarity and is charged with kindness, it communicates respect. Whether or not the person who asked for your participation responds with the same respect and kindness is not your responsibility. You are responsible for only your behavior.

Giving to others is rewarding, but when it is done from a place of obligation or insincerity, it creates negativity for you and others.

Leaving room for self-nourishment is important when giving to others. By replenishing your energy, you strengthen your body, mind, and spirit; which allows you to give from a place of stability.

The "Super Woman" role

If you are a woman, you are familiar with the responsibility many women take on to fulfill the "super-woman" role. No matter how tired or busy she might be, a woman is expected to give as a wife, mother, daughter, friend, member of the community, work place, and the world. A woman's capacity to give can extend far beyond the day-to-day responsibilities when she goes out of her way to give her time, in any capacity to others. More often than not, she ends up exhausted from a lack of self-nourishment.

Guilt at not fulfilling other's expectations, doing something even if you don't want to, fearing judgment of your capacities, self-criticism, or comparisons to other women weaken your spirit. You have nothing to prove to anyone. You know that you are capable to give much to others, but if you are not ready or available to do something or don't want to do it, it is important to say so.

I am not talking about everyday situations that require you to take responsibility such as going to work or tending your children, I am talking about situations that make you unhappy because self-nourishment is not taking place—specifically, situations that create imbalance or negativity in your life.

Changing the course of your path

More often than not, you are able to change the course of your path by making choices that are aligned with your intentions. To do this, it is necessary to be clear on what your intentions are and initiate action from there.

It doesn't serve any purpose to complain about a current situation you may be unhappy with. It is more productive to spend time in introspection, and from there discover all viable options. Let's say you are unhappy with your current job situation. You can look for another job in a different department within the same company, you can look for a job in a different company, you can go back to school and choose a career change, or you can open your own company. Complaining about a situation or a person only feeds the negativity that already exists around it. Think of all your options and begin to set intentions toward a different reality, then, initiate action.

How can situations or people support your transformation?

As we all know, change is the only constant. We experience change in the weather, in our bodies, as each season passes, when new friendships arrive and old ones depart, when our work situation shifts, when people we love pass, and as our children grow.

It is also important to remember that every situation will eventually change or dissolve, and that people arrive only for a period of time, some short and others long.

Regardless of how long a situation is part of your life, you have the opportunity to make the best of every situation. Situations and people allow for self-awareness when you question the purpose and lessons for their presence. When a situation or a person represents a challenge, ask yourself, "What is the purpose of this situation? What is this person teaching me?"

Situations and people arrive to heal you, teach you, and guide you. As one situation resolves, another appears with new lessons, people, and opportunities for more transformation. When you become aware of this, your perception of the situation changes and you begin to view it as an opportunity for self-growth.

As your perception shifts, the situation may change or you seek change. In other cases, situations dissolve as soon as you learn the lessons behind them.

There is always something to learn from a situation or a person. It could be that a situation arrives to teach you to set boundaries and become clearer on whether or not you want to participate. In certain occasions, your participation might be imperative or necessary, allowing you to practice compassion, selflessness and unconditional love through service to others —you have the opportunity to treat another person the way you would like to be treated if you were going through similar circumstances.

When you are in a situation you are unhappy with, you can ask yourself, "Does this situation promote my well-being? Does this situation match my beliefs?"

Feelings of guilt and punishment exist around the belief that you must experience discomfort as a way of sacrifice by participating in or accepting unwanted situations.

You are not here to suffer. You are here to evolve spiritually, to know yourself better, and set boundaries based on that knowledge. You can never please everyone, nor can you expect others to think or act like you do. You cannot choose how others must feel, but you can choose your feelings. You can consciously decide how to approach someone or a situation and maintain your boundaries.

If your "no" comes from a place of kindness, there is no reason for the other person to be offended or angry. If the person you are saying "no" to is offended or takes your "no" personally, he must take responsibility for that. As long as you honor your boundaries and express them with kindness and respect, you are taking responsibility for your part.

Unavailability or disagreement can be expressed without negativity. Simply say, "No, thank you!" There is no need to elaborate or offer complicated explanations or justifications.

Our values and priorities

No matter what your role—parent, business man, working two jobs, single woman, someone famous, not working, caring for someone ill, divorced—you strive to live a life of balance and stability, a life where joy is a constant. If that weren't the case, you wouldn't be reading this book. But how can you create such life in a world full of schedules, commitments, deadlines, distractions, and expectations? It is simple: clarity. Being clear, honoring and prioritizing your values is important when it comes to creating a life of balance. A value has three attributes: it inspires, strengthens, and promotes. A value inspires you to move forward and opens you to expansion and creativity. It strengthens your spirit, igniting your Being with positive energy and enthusiasm. It promotes harmony and peace, creating self-transformation.

You set boundaries by knowing and prioritizing your values. A balanced life is created when you actively choose to bring into your life people and activities that cultivate your values. Your actions must match your values in order to create balance.

Consistency is an important value to nourish during this process. When you initiate action, consistency is imperative to transform unhealthy patterns.

The exercise below can help you become clearer on your values and prioritize them. It will also help you think of the actions that you can initiate to change unhealthy patterns or create a more balanced life.

When doing the exercise, I suggest that you include the following areas: spiritual, physical (health and wellness), relationships, financial (wealth, prosperity and abundance) and career (purpose, self-realization, service) for a clear perspective on the values you hold for each area. Like the exercises in previous chapters, take your time, be honest with your answers, and have fun while doing it.

"Prioritizing values" exercise

Area of my life: _____.

Example: Relationships

My values

Important values, related to (area of my life) are:

_____.

(What are the values you cherish in that area?)

Example: Important values related to relationships, are love, friendship, company, sharing, learning, and giving.

My priorities

It is very important to me that: _____.

(Write statements that describe what is important to you. Make sure that each statement is written in order of importance).

Example:

Priority 1: It is very important to spend quality time as a family every day.

Priority 2: It is very important to go out with my husband on a date once a week.

Priority 3: It is very important to meet with my friends at least once a month.

Obstacles

Possible obstacles are: _____.

(Write any obstacle or obstacles that may impede you from accomplishing any of your priorities).

Example:

Obstacle to priority 1: There is not enough time; we are all so busy.

Obstacle to priority 2: We are really tired, and it is often hard to synch our schedules and go out at night.

Obstacle to priority 3: My friends are always busy.

Setting boundaries

My new action is: _____.

(Write a statement that sets boundaries and an action that will help you change an unhealthy pattern or create more balance in that area).

Example:

Boundaries related to priority 1:

Instead of talking on the phone with my friends, I will dedicate that time to be with my family.

Or: Instead of watching TV or playing video games, we will take a half-hour walk outside and talk about something of interest to us.

Or: Twice a week, I will get up earlier to prepare and have breakfast with my son before he goes to school.

Or: When I cook at night, I will invite my children to cook with me so that we can all participate and spend quality time together.

Or: Every night before my daughter goes to sleep, I will spend time asking her about her day and telling her about mine.

Or: We will play a board game after dinner.

Boundary related to priority 2:

I will hire a reliable babysitter at least two nights a month so that I can have a date night with my husband.

Boundary related to priority 3:

I will call my friends in advance to have a get together once a month; we will rotate homes, and each person will bring a dish to share.

Knowing your limitations, setting boundaries, and matching your actions with your values will allow you to create a life of balance. Change, new beginnings, transformation, or spiritual growth happens when you take responsibility for your part in any situation. Hiding behind excuses such as lack of time, not enough resources, or other people's behavior perpetuates the patterns that block your potential from full expression.

Use your values as guidelines in any situation. Allow each person who arrives in your life to teach you something. Life gives you the opportunity for self-discovery through everything you experience, so welcome all of it with flexibility and open arms. This flexibility will create space for your perception of the world and life to change. As your consciousness rises, it affects the collective consciousness as well.

Suggestions

Set boundaries.

When you feel discomfort around a person or a situation, if the time and space allows for it, speak up about your discomfort. Try to express what is bothering you without negativity, avoiding attacks or blame. It is important to take responsibility for your feelings without transferring negativity. An example is to use a statement like: "I don't feel comfortable with this." or "This is not ok with me, and would like to look into a different option to resolve it."

Practice saying "no, thank you."

If a situation arrives where you are not able, willing or ready to participate, practice saying "no, thank you," without elaborating on your answer. This is a beautiful practice that supports individuality and self-respect.

Write your values.

Write some of the most important values you hold on paper, sticky notes, or index cards, and place them around your house, car, or office place to remind you of those values.

Create a "new life plan" calendar.

On a calendar, write a value per month that you would like to concentrate on, as well as the actions you are committed to initiate that support that value.

Commit to doing something that nourishes you.

Self-nourishment is necessary to recharge your energy. Daily if not weekly, commit to doing something that inspires, strengthens, or promotes positivism in you.

PRACTICE 5
PRESENCE: THE MANIFESTATION OF CONSCIOUSNESS

Transform your life through presence.

Known also as self-realization, awakening, awareness, or enlightenment, consciousness manifests through attributes such as wholeness, pureness, profound love, detachment, truth, gratitude, peace, joy, and compassion. For many of us, consciousness is experienced only in moments that allow us a taste of what pure joy and complete freedom might feel like.

These *conscious moments* can increase in frequency and last longer when we take on practices that promote well-being such as silence, self-observation and *presence*.

When you are present, your senses are alert, you are open to anything that life may bring. There is no fear, or suffering, and your actions carry an energy frequency that reflects peace and balance.

Presence, or the practice of being present, can easily be accessed through outward meditation (using aspects of your daily life to attain awareness and from there initiate transformation), in the form of participation or communion. Communion comes from the Latin word *commūniō*, which means, "general participation or sharing in common."

It can be said that every time your participation is charged with presence, you are practicing a form of meditation and also experiencing a conscious moment, because your actions are aligned with *consciousness*. We can also refer to this as "conscious participation."

Presence is a powerful tool for raising your level of consciousness and is available all the time. Practicing presence doesn't cost anything; it requires only of your willingness to be receptive, so that transformation can occur within you.

Some examples of situations where consciousness can be raised by practicing presence are:

During conversations, giving the person who is speaking space to talk and express his point of view. This strengthens your capacity to detach from your own views and listen without interrupting.

When a situation changes unexpectedly. While you cannot control a situation, you can always control how you approach it. When your approach is charged with presence, your experience of the situation transforms, because you are viewing it from a place of openness and non-resistance. You can practice presence during situations that require patience and flexibility, such as getting stuck in traffic, a cancellation on a flight, or a medical emergency, to name a few.

Heartfelt gestures of kindness toward another Being allow you to practice selflessness and bring about one of the most beautiful ways to support consciousness: service to others. The smallest gesture of kindness has the potential to transform positively someone's experience, feelings, or perceptions, especially when is expressed without expecting anything in return.

Every time you express gratitude, you arrive immediately at a place of presence, because gratitude is born from awareness. Awareness is manifested in your capacity to acknowledge and be grateful for the value that everything holds.

How can situations heal you?

Every situation can serve as a source for transformation and self-healing. For this to happen, a high degree of presence is necessary.

Presence creates space for clarity to exist, and clarity is vital to make decisions or take action without negativity (such as blame or guilt).

When a situation arrives, the first response is usually to label it as positive or negative. Labeling limits you to your own view, but presence allows you to see the many sides that a situation holds. If you label a situation as negative, you automatically make a decision against it instead of letting it show you its potential.

How many times have you perceived a situation as negative and realized days, months, or even years later that because of the situation, you became stronger, more compassionate, more flexible, more forgiving, or more aware? Situations have the power to affect others who haven't even been involved. How often have you heard someone say that she became more aware when learning about someone else's approach to a situation?

Every situation presents exactly what you need for your growth at a specific moment. If you miss the lessons of a situation, the lessons will manifest again and again, disguised in many forms, until you become aware of them and take action toward transformation.

The teachings are not a punishment, and their purpose is never to cause suffering. Their purpose is to grant you opportunities where consciousness can manifest within. How you use these opportunities is up to you.

Resistance to a situation comes from the need to control an outcome, fear of the unknown or attachment to the "familiar." Resisting, opposing, struggling, fighting and blocking, are all attributes of negativity, and take you sooner or later to the same place: suffering.

There is a difference between suffering and sadness. Suffering leaves you confused, fearful, and it blocks you from making a healthy choice or finding a liable solution. It serves as an excuse to blame, punish, create drama, withdraw, justify, attack, or judge, instead of taking responsibility for your personal growth.

Sadness is expressed from a place of peace and acceptance. When you are sad, you also understand the possibilities behind a situation, you know that everything passes, and you trust the situation exists to contribute to your well-being. Accepting doesn't mean lack of action; healthy and fruitful action can be initiated only when you accept a situation, as without acceptance, you cannot move on or progress.

There is nothing wrong with expressing sadness, and tears are a healthy way to express and release. If you cry, be present with your crying, and allow yourself to express your sadness through it. If you are present, you will experience peace, deep love, and compassion.

As sad as a situation might be, it appears in your life to bring you clarity, to communicate something, to empower you, to inspire you, to empower or inspire others, to protect you, to create awareness, or to create space for other things or people to arrive. Sometimes a situation arrives as the "push" you need to take action and change the course of your life.

Anything you resist will keep you stuck and obstruct your transformation. Life needs your openness and cooperation to teach you how you can heal yourself and others through every event that arrives in your life.

As your level of consciousness raises through space, silence, self-observation, self-knowledge and presence, you become more flexible, and your approach to life reflects that flexibility. Your capacity to acknowledge the many sides of any given situation expands, and your approach is clear, solid, healthy, and peaceful.

Welcoming a situation requires your complete trust. Trust in knowing that the situation will heal you, not harm you. Trust in knowing that if you allow it to be, you are consciously participating in a work of love: your own spiritual evolution. This is awakening. This is the manifestation of consciousness within you.

Lao Tzu said, "Be content with what you have, rejoice in the way things are. When you realize there is nothing lacking, the whole world belongs to you."

Allowing situations to show you what is needed in order for transformation to happen will bring you closer to a state where life is not about suffering but about celebration, inspiration, evolution, and joy.

The exercise below will help you obtain clarity through the practice of presence in any situation that causes you stress, discomfort, fear, suffering, or negativity. Every time you write something, stay alert, practice presence, be aware of your feelings, be honest, and listen to your intuition.

"Presence and clarity" exercise

Step 1: Identify the situation.

Example:

Situation: I just got fired.

Step 2: Practice presence.

(Be present by welcoming whatever is going on, and try not to label it as positive or negative).

Spend a few minutes in silence, listen to your breathing, do nothing. Practice non-resistance by welcoming the situation as is. As you breathe slowly, repeat, "I just got fired… this will pass," allowing any feelings to manifest. Keep repeating, "I just got fired… this will pass." When you are more relaxed and feel ready for introspection, proceed to the next step.

Step 3: Identify fears, your options, and the benefits.

My fears are: _____.

(Write down all your fears about the situation).

Example:

I am afraid of not being able to find another job soon.

I am afraid to lose my health benefits.

My options are: _____.

(Write down all the possibilities and options you have in the situation).

Example:

Option 1: I can look for another job.

Option 2: I can go back to school.

Option 3: I can open my own company.

Option 4: I can stay unemployed.

The benefits are: _____.

(Write down all the benefits that might come with each option).

Example:

Option 1: I can look for another job.

Benefits: Meeting new people. Working for a great company. Learning something new. Asking for a higher salary.

Option 2: I can go back to school.

Benefits: Learning something new. Meeting new people. Getting the certification that will allow me to teach English abroad. Taking a break from work.

Option 3: I can open my own company.

Benefits: I can be my own boss. I can benefit the economy by creating jobs for others. I can participate on every aspect of starting a business and apply my ideas to it.

Option 4: I can stay unemployed.

Benefits: I have the flexibility and time to exercise, travel, or volunteer at the local hospital.

Step 4: Find the lessons behind the situation.

Ask yourself, what do I feel this situation wants to teach me or give me?

(Write down all the lessons you feel this situation has arrived to teach you or give you. Be present as you inquire, and write as many statements as possible).

Example:

I feel this situation arrived to:

Teach me that jobs come and go, that nothing is permanent.

Give me the opportunity to get a new job and the possibility of a higher position with a higher salary.

Teach me not to take for granted the things I have when I have them.

Give me clarity to see what I want and don't want out of this situation.

Step 5: Write down your actions.

(Based on your options, their benefits and knowing the lessons behind the situation, write down a course of action that will support the knowledge you have acquired. This is a "mission statement" that clearly states your new intention and the actions necessary to manifest it).

Example:

"I want to look for another job, but I also want to get a certification to teach abroad."

Action: I will apply for a part-time position that will allow me the time to get the teaching certification I want. While I look for another position, I will take advantage of the free time I have to exercise and reorganize my garage.

Suggestions

Spend time in contemplative meditation.

Contemplative meditation is a powerful practice that helps you exercise non-judgment, by observing what is around you without labeling it as positive or negative. It also helps you realize the power of presence as you learn the art of "doing nothing." One of the greatest benefits of contemplative meditation is the realization that you can access consciousness at any time and in any place by just "Being." Sit in a comfortable position as long as you are able or willing to, and observe everything around you. Try not to label any objects, only observe. As you observe become aware of each breath, be present with it. This practice might feel uncomfortable at first; you might experience impatience or irritability. This is normal, because we are used to be constantly in motion or occupied. Stay as long as possible with any feelings that arise, trying not to judge your feelings. When you are ready, resume the practice.

Practice presence by observing nature.

Whenever possible, take a walk outside. Feel your body as you walk, try to walk slow. Pay attention at every color, noise, shape and texture in nature. As you observe, acknowledge the abundance around you, the perfection within a flower, the beautiful sound of a bird, the agility of a squirrel, the magnificence of a mountain, the incredible feeling of the air touching your face.

Listen carefully.

When you listen to someone else, be present. Listen without interrupting; give the person who is speaking your full attention. Try to listen without judging or thinking of the statement you would like to respond with. Simply listen and offer that person space to Be.

PRACTICE 6
EXPRESSING GRATITUDE: ATTRACTS ABUNDANCE

Acknowledging abundance welcomes it; expressing gratitude attracts it.

Gratitude is experienced every time you acknowledge someone or something for its value, beauty, benefit, utility, blessings, power, or strength. This acknowledgment carries energy frequencies that signal to life your openness to receive; this is how abundance is manifested. Gratefulness has the power to attract in abundance the things you value and are grateful for.

Abundance and gratitude are two aspects of life that are always interconnected. Life is full, never empty, and there is always enough for everyone. Life expresses abundance as a continuous and never-ending flow of love. Abundance occurs as an exchange between life's intelligence and you—every time you express appreciation for life, it thanks you back in one way or another.

The first step to attracting abundance into your life is to become aware of the many forms in which abundance is manifested. In the world of form, money and material things are expressions of abundance. Spiritually speaking, abundance is expressed in nature, the universe, and your Being.

Recognizing abundance in nature

Nature is one of the most precious manifestations of abundance. There is abundance in the rain, the oceans, the grass; each tree holds an abundance of leaves, flowers, or fruits. You can find in any landscape abundance of shapes and colors. Abundance within the universe is prodigious with planets and galaxies (think of the four hundred billion stars in the Milky Way alone).

Any time you feel a lack of abundance in your life, observe nature, and let it show you how vast and prosperous life is. Life is telling you, "There is enough for everyone."

Recognizing abundance in your daily life

You can recognize countless manifestations of abundance in your day-to-day life and use this as a practice to express gratitude, for example: a trip to a store can be a great opportunity to acknowledge abundance, as each aisle holds an endless amount of items that have been invented for your comfort, enjoyment or to simplify your life: clothing, decorative items, gardening tools, toys and electronics, to name a few.

In supermarkets, fruits and vegetables are displayed beautifully, having traveled hundreds, and sometimes thousands, of miles to be consumed and enhance your health and well-being.

There are plenty of items in your household to be grateful for: appliances, electronics, books, keepsakes and art.

Your body is one of the most beautiful representations of abundance, holding millions of cells, arteries, and pores. Each organ is amazing; the brain alone has more than one hundred billion nerve cells.

Two attributes of gratitude are honor and respect, and both imply recognition, caring for, and consideration. From the smallest most seemingly-insignificant item, to the biggest, everything you are and have deserves appreciation. Your life is a reflection of your capacity to appreciate, honor, and respect all there is, inside of you and around you.

Every time you become aware of the many manifestations of abundance in your life, express gratitude toward *all* you are and have at this moment.

Another important aspect related to attracting abundance is trust. Trusting implies letting go of expectations. Knowing that there is enough of everything for everybody, allows life to show us in what capacity we are ready to receive.

Everyone is part of the flow of abundance and deserves it, but not everyone feels deserving. To attract abundance, believe that you deserve it, just like everyone else.

Complaining

Complaining is the opposite of gratitude. Complains arise out of discontent, dissatisfaction, or simply the need to create drama. Every time you complain, you allow negativity to be part of your environment and your Being. Complaining is a hurtful and damaging activity that drains your precious energy needed to raise awareness, the only place where transformation occurs.

When you complain, you resist. You are out of sync with what is. You are saying "no" to life, and life will reply with the same negation. This is the universal law of abundance. When you complain, abundance is manifested in the form of negativity, attracting more negativity. To attract the opposite, become aware of those times you complain, and transform the complaint into a statement that produces positive feelings.

Every time you make a conscious effort to replace a complaint with a statement of gratitude, your levels of energy rise, changing the chemistry in your body, and you attract more of what you are grateful for. You contribute to your own spiritual evolution, and you create a positive effect in the world.

I have observed first-hand how my mother's kindness and patience is a source for transformation. She has faced extremely challenging situations but has always come out of them with more strength and wisdom. It has been an honor to have known so closely a person whom capacity to be compassionate and empathetic toward others inspires everyone who meets her. She appreciates everything she comes in contact with, views every situation as an opportunity to grow, and lives with enthusiasm and passion—always cooperating, never resisting. To me, her life is lived fully!

One time at the airport, her flight was cancelled at the last minute. While other passengers were angry by the situation, she calmly walked to the counter to request options about other flights. The person at the counter was annoyed by the passengers' complaints, and he must have felt my mom's nonresistance, because he responded to her with the same kindness with which she approached him. He probably couldn't believe that there was one person who wasn't complaining to him—to the contrary, she was cooperating by being patient and showing him respect. He immediately started looking for alternative flights and went out of his way to help her. He said, "I can put you on a flight with our partner airline, there is only one seat available, but you must run because the flight is about to leave. I will call the flight attendant in charge, to let her know that you will be boarding, they will be waiting for you." My mother got on that flight and made it to her destination on time.

The airline worker didn't make the decision to cancel the flight; he was probably just as frustrated as the passengers were with the whole situation. No one could have changed the fact that the flight was cancelled, but everyone had the power to choose how to experience the situation. My mother's kindness and patience gave the airline worker the space to respond to her in the same way. Her empathy allowed him to give empathy.

A cancellation or an opening on another flight wouldn't have made a difference in my mother's state, but her detachment allowed her to be free of the outcome, and her kindness caused a positive effect on another person. Collaboration, nonresistance, kindness, flexibility are values that welcome situations without negativity and have the power to affect you and others.

Complaining can turn into a habit. Chronic complainers do it with such frequency that they become unconscious of it.

A common form of negativity is anger. Some people excuse their complaining by saying that complaining is a way to let out anger. There are many ways to release anger and complaining is one of them. We are not trying to release negativity; our purpose is to transform negativity into positivism. By transforming it, we dissolve it. Once we dissolve it, there is nothing to release.

Exercise, yoga, a healthy hobby, meditation, prayer, silence, healthy communication, and introspection are actions that can allow you to transform any form of negativity into awareness, balance, and peace. When awareness is raised, it is easier to pinpoint the times when negativity is being promoted and transform it. Affirmations and actions underlined by kindness are always healthier than negativity.

Releasing anger or dissatisfaction through complaining can seem easier than taking time to exercise awareness in order to change behavior, but complaining or whining produces negativity beyond the complainer, harming him as well as his environment. In reality, insecurity hides behind the release of anger to reinforce an illusory sense of power. This illusory sense of power is momentary and happens only on the surface. Spiritual strength and true power are acquired when you are capable of transforming negativity into an attribute that promotes well-being. The effects of positive transformation are felt by everyone involved.

Situations don't always work the way you want or expect, but every situation has a reason for its existence. Nothing happens by mistake. Life flows in perfect order, and when you value and honor everything as is, you honor life, the intelligence behind it and yourself.

"Transform complaining into gratitude" exercise

When you catch yourself complaining, write the complaint, and below it, write a statement that transforms the complaint into a statement of gratitude. Write as many statements of gratitude as you can, beginning with the words, "I am grateful for."

Complaint:

_____.

I am grateful for:

_____.

Examples:

Complaint:

"I hate this weather; it has been raining for a week."

Statements of gratitude:

"I am grateful for the rain; it represents abundance and it is necessary for the preservation of life."

"I am grateful for the sound of the rain; it is soothing and relaxing."

"I am grateful for this weather; it is the perfect weather to visit a museum."

"I am grateful for this weather; it makes me appreciate the sunny days."

Complaint:

"The lady at the supermarket is always angry."

Statements of gratitude:

"I am grateful for the fact that we have supermarkets."

"I am grateful for people who work during the weekends and make it possible for me to buy what I need at the supermarket."

"I am grateful for the opportunity to treat the lady at the supermarket with kindness and respect."

After transforming complaints into gratitude statements, take ownership for your feelings and your actions. Let's look at the supermarket attendant's complaint: "The lady at the supermarket is always angry." The attendant's behavior might be unkind and creates negativity that affects customers, but let's not forget that the attendant's state of anger and what she does with it is her responsibility, not the customer's. The attendant has the choice to act differently. When the customer expresses negativity through a complaint, he creates more negativity on top of the negativity created already by the attendant. Now we have two people swimming in a pool of negativity. Can you see how negativity can be contagious and cause damage to both sides? If the customer transforms the complaint into a statement of gratitude, the customer raises awareness inward as well as outward. The customer can take this opportunity even further by acting with kindness toward the attendant. Whether or not the attendant decides to respond to the customer with kindness is her choice and should not be of concern to the customer. We are responsible only for our consciousness, not for anyone else's. In this case, the customer was able to transform the complaint into a statement of gratitude, and by using kindness in his language and action toward the attendant, supported this transformation.

Attracting abundance

To begin attracting abundance, know that everything you attract is a manifestation of the intelligence that exists inside and outside of you. This intelligence speaks the language of energy that exists everywhere and in everything. This intelligence is perfect and whole. You are it, and the world is it.

In his book *Power versus Force*, David Hawkins, MD, PhD, presents an interesting technique to calibrate levels of energy. Hawkins proposes that through kinesiology, the scientific study of human movement, levels of energy can be measured on anything from a book to a statement, food, a thought or a word. He presents a consciousness chart that groups levels of energy. Levels below 200 obstruct life, and levels above 200 promote life. Guilt, fear, and anger are some of the energy levels below 200; willingness, acceptance, love, joy, and peace are some of the energy levels above 200.

Everything you do, say, think, or feel carries energy frequencies that can empower or limit you. Negativity blocks life intelligence from expressing freely through you and stops you from using your full potential.

You are communicating every moment what you want and how you want it by using the language of abundance to attract it. You attract situations, people, and things that resonate with the level of frequency you carry within.

Some activities that raise levels of energy include creating clean and open spaces in your home or work place that communicate balance; having people around you who enhance your life with love, flexibility, and joy; eating foods that nurture your body; any practice that centers, relaxes, or calms you (excluding drugs or alcohol) such as silence, meditation, prayer, and yoga; the practice of self-observation; being in a state of presence; laughing; expressing gratitude; and giving to others without expecting anything in return.

Anything that promotes growth and awareness raises your energy frequency and therefore your level of consciousness.

Giving

Our existence is supported by an exchange wherein every organism gives and receives to maintain the flow of life. Life's main characteristic is abundance, manifesting in situations where giving is done without any expectation and with the intention to promote the well-being of others. Conscious giving is done without announcing it or hoping for it to be noticed. It is done from a place of "wanting to" rather than "having to."

The exchange produces well-being for all those who participate; the giver may experience detachment, selflessness, service and kindness; the receiver may experience humility, allowance, gratitude, and joy.

Opportunities to give are countless and most of them are free. Having money is not necessary for giving to happen, and in many instances, your participation and gift of time may hold a greater value or have a more powerful impact than money.

You don't have to think of an extraordinary cause to be of service to others, as giving is extraordinary at any capacity. You can make a big difference by giving in your home, your community, your children's school, or your work place. Giving can be doing a house chore without being asked to, spending quality time with a friend, supporting a family member during a challenging situation, helping out a neighbor, and volunteering.

Money as a tool

Money is the material representation of value and most powerful ruler in the world of form. It isn't negative, bad or dirty—to the contrary, from a spiritual perspective, money can be used as a tool to raise awareness. Ultimately, your perception of money determines how you use it and how you attract it.

When money is perceived as a means to an end, your ticket to freedom, or your happiness provider, sooner or later you will discover that you can never have enough. As soon as you reach a certain status, you need more, and if you don't have "enough," you are constantly preoccupied and disappointed.

It is easy to get caught up in the desire to have lots of money, especially in a society that perceives money as power and freedom, but we all know that true power and true freedom can only be attained from within. The power and freedom that money may provide is superficial and temporary, because money is form, and form always passes, changes or dissolves. Freedom is expressed in your capacity to enjoy material things for their benefits and see them go without being affected in any way.

Respect is a value that can be practiced when using money. Treating money and those things money can buy with respect promotes a sense of appreciation. You are saying with your actions, "I know you are a helpful tool; I appreciate you and treat you with respect." The way you treat money communicates how you feel about it. By keeping your wallet and bank accounts in order, paying off any debt, not consuming items you don't need, you confirm to life your willingness to appreciate money at any level, even a penny.

Giving and sharing money with others promotes its flow, allowing abundance to manifest through the amount of money that flows and through the many other values that ignite from sharing it— detachment, service, love, joy, kindness, and compassion.

You can truly enjoy money when you don't empower it but empower your spirituality through it. It can teach you spiritual freedom. You can have money in abundance and still be humble; you can use money to share and provide for others in need. When you use it as a tool to transform, it does exactly that and is reproduced with the same intention.

You aren't here to experience scarcity; you are here to attract abundance and enjoy it. Abundance is reflected in your capacity to see life as an endless opportunity to Be at your full potential, to show appreciation toward all things, to share all you are and all you have with others without expecting anything in return, and to use money as a tool for transformation. These actions signal to life your readiness to receive more. Life delivers in return, always knowing exactly what you need and how you need it.

The language of abundance

Thoughts and words have immense power. Each thought that you hold or word that you say carries with it energy frequencies that affect you and others in a positive or negative way.

To attract abundance, it is necessary to transform negative thought patterns into affirmations that use the language of abundance.

The language of abundance is not taught at any school, nor can you buy a "Dictionary of Abundance." This is a self-taught language, where you must invest time and effort toward learning it.

Negative thought patters are either inherited from others or produced by the ego, becoming part of a belief system.

You are communicating negativity when a thought or word weakens, limits, resists, excludes, attacks, judges, or blames you or others, creating feelings of guilt, superiority, fear, anger, or suffering.

How do you transform negative thoughts and words into positive ones? It is a process that requires paying close attention to the way you speak, pinpointing negative thoughts that are repeated often, transforming each thought into one that promotes positive feelings and supports your intentions, and practicing by speaking the language of abundance as much as possible. The more you use it, the more those negative patterns will be transformed into positive ones.

The language of abundance uses words like *trust, believe, know, willing, prefer, enough, grateful, love, cherish, kind, generous, loving, sweet, creative, beautiful, giving, supportive, can, healthy, strong, responsible,* and *fun.*

The steps below will guide you through transforming negative thought patterns into affirmations that use the language of abundance. Again, the more you practice the easier it gets. You will find yourself speaking it more and more with little or no effort.

Step 1: Observe your language.

Identify negative thoughts you would like to transform. Again, thoughts that weaken, limit, resist, exclude, attack, judge or blame must be replaced by thoughts that empower, allow, include, support, accept, love, or inspire.

Step 2: Transform your language.

Once you have identified unhealthy thoughts you use repeatedly, you can begin to transform them by using the language of abundance. Negativity negates, positivism affirms. Let's look at a couple of examples.

Negative statement:

"I don't have enough money to go out tonight."

Language of abundance:

"I prefer to use the money I have another time."

Negative statement:

"I am so fat; it is my fault for eating so much food."

Language of abundance:

"I am grateful for the delicious food I can eat. I love my body and want to be healthy. I trust in my willpower to eat smaller portions of food. The next time I eat, I will exercise this power to promote my well-being."

Negative statement:

"My sister is so lazy and irresponsible.

Language of abundance:

"My sister is a human being who deserves my respect. She can be loving, kind, and sweet."

Step 3: Use the language of abundance.

Speak the language of abundance as much as possible. Practice anytime and anywhere you can, especially if you are in the company of others. Using statements that support positivism and well-being creates an avalanche effect in those around you. Positivism is contagious and in many cases ignites awareness in others.

Repeating positive statements in the presence of others has the power to ignite transformation in those who might not be aware of the benefit or value something holds. Growing up, I heard my mother speak beautifully about rain. Every time it rained, she said, "I love the sound of the rain, it is so calming" or "Thank God it is raining, the plants need it" or "Isn't the smell of wet dirt so nice?" Hearing these statements often helped me to be aware of the magnificence and benefits of the rain. If the moment and the situation allows for it, when you are in the presence of others, share your positive outlook in life.

Recognize and appreciate abundance everywhere you go. To attract abundance, realize where and how it manifests and extend gratitude toward it.

Every time you recognize abundance, repeat statements like, "I am amazed at the abundance of fruits and vegetables in the supermarket" or "I love the variety of colors and shapes at the flower shop" or "There are so many people trying to get fit and be healthier at the gym this morning."

Greet abundance, and life will greet you with the same.

Make a dream box

Find a box made out of any material; decorate it if you want to. The box must communicate things that are important to you: beauty, simplicity, elegance, fun, diversity, etc.

Put inside the box anything that represents an intention, a dream, or something you want to attract into your life. Include things that symbolize or remind you of a loved one, empowering times when you accomplished something important, or something that means spiritual growth for you.

Anytime you think of something you want to attract to your life, write it down on a piece of paper and put it in your dream box. If you see a photo on a magazine that represents something you want, cut it out and put it in the box. Write down what you want to accomplish, and put it in the box. Insert in the box everything you wish to be and attract.

Every time you put something in the box, express a statement of gratitude related to the intention or desire. For example, let's say that you want to travel to Japan. As you are writing your intention, think of the times you have traveled and say, "I am grateful for … " ("the times I have traveled" or "the beautiful memories I have from my travels" or "the wonderful people I have met during my travels.").

Clarity is important when you are communicating your intentions to the universal intelligence. The more specific you are, the better.

Confusion emerges when you aren't clear about what you want and how you want it. A clear statement regarding your intention to travel to Japan can be, "I would like to have the necessary amount of money to travel to Japan for at least fifteen days comfortably and without scarcity within the next year."

No negativity is allowed inside of your dream box—only positive thoughts, words, or intentions that you already have and would like to continue to have or you wish to add to your life.

There is enough for everybody. Abundance arrives when you trust that you will always have what is necessary and right for you. It doesn't serve you to compare yourself with others, as each person travels life's journey in a unique way. When you acknowledge the abundance around and in you, are grateful for it, and use the language of abundance, you attract it.

Suggestions

Express gratitude.

Every time you become aware of the presence of abundance, express gratitude. There is so much to be grateful for. You can express gratitude for your legs when you walk, for food when you eat, for love when you kiss a loved one, for the opportunity to attend a fun event, for technology when you use a computer, for your health when you breathe, for your eyes when you see beauty.

Transform complaint into gratitude.

When you become aware of complaining, take the opportunity to transform the complaint into a statement that communicates gratitude. Keep a gratitude journal where you write the gratitude statements that replaced the complaints.

Give and share with others whenever possible.

You don't have to have money to give or share; you can share your time, energy, company, or talents. Think of all the ways in which you can serve others by giving or sharing, and use any opportunity to do so. Intentions are great, but to manifest them, they must be accompanied by action.

Show respect to everything you have.

Including money, show respect to everyone and everything that you have or is presented to you. We often take things and people for granted, forgetting all the beautiful gifts we receive from them. You can show respect by caring for all the material things you have, by treating people with kindness, by keeping your surroundings clean and orderly and by being kind toward yourself.

PRACTICE 7
UNFOLDING YOUR INTENTIONS: THE REALIZATION OF PURPOSE

In the midst of any situation, live fully.

What is my purpose? And how can I fulfill it? Millions of people ask themselves these questions. Trying to find the answers often becomes a life project consumed by time, energy, and money, ending in frustration, when the search reveals nothing but the same routines or habitual patterns.

The search ends when you realize that you never *find* a purpose, you *create* it, and it is manifested through your intentions and actions. Intentions are the main ingredient in creating a purpose.

Why limit this journey to only one purpose? All of us share two qualities: our humanity and our spirituality. As a spiritual Being, you share a purpose with all other humans: your spiritual evolution. Paradoxically, this evolution is possible only through your experiences as a human, and without these experiences, you would remain in the same state. As a human, you are here to fulfill many purposes, and each one is valuable and necessary for your growth and the growth of the world.

It takes a vision, an intention, a project, or an idea to create a purpose, but its realization can only be experienced through actions. Purpose doesn't knock on the door or show up in the mail; it is created out of awareness.

Purpose can come about through any situation. For example, in the workplace, your purpose can be to promote an environment of respect among your coworkers by having an attitude of collaboration. Another purpose can be to practice patience and flexibility when an important outcome on a project doesn't turn out the way you expected. At home, your purpose can be to create an environment of peace by expressing disagreement with kindness instead of negativity or to spend more quality time together as a family. Your purpose in the community can be to share your gifts and talents at your children's school by volunteering. The sky is the limit. You may create daily, monthly, yearly or life purposes. Anything from taking care of your body by exercising to changing careers or taking on a new hobby can become a purpose.

Spiritually speaking, we all share a common denominator: our spirit; therefore, collectively we share the same purpose: spiritual evolution. We are all a reflection of the same energy and intelligence through which we connect to all other human beings. Whether you call it Buddha, Jesus, God, or Life, this intelligence manifests through your Being, which encompasses spirit (consciousness) and form (body).

Many people look for something magical that can transform their life and end up feeling disappointed if they don't find it. Frustration, disappointment, and depression are often the result of attributing salvation to a purpose that may arrive "someday." Happiness can be experienced through the fulfillment of a purpose, but this usually passes when the purpose changes or ends or when we are no longer satisfied by it. On the other hand, spiritual awareness, or self realization is experienced from within, not as a result of an outcome; and in this state, true joy is a constant.

How do you know whether or not a purpose that promotes growth for you and others is manifesting? When you experience feelings of joy and enthusiasm, life is expressed through you as creativity and inspiration, others are affected positively by your actions, situations flow with ease, your environment is healthy and peaceful, you live a life of service, and abundance manifests in your life. Negative feelings such as anger, boredom, confusion, aloneness, indifference, dependency, frustration, stress, and fear are the result of a life away from purpose. These feelings are a sign that old patterns are blocking life from flowing with ease through you. They are indicators that change is necessary to create new outcomes, receive new things, and transform your life and the lives of others.

Changing a perception from "a life purpose" to "a life of many purposes" or "I have to find my purpose" to "I want to become aware of my intentions and commit to match them with my actions" allows you to live a life of unlimited possibilities. You begin to live a life where you become the only one responsible for its outcome, and this is a reflection of integrity and strength.

Your participation is all that is needed to create a life of purpose. When you become aware of an intention and listen to your intuition, you establish communication with a conscious intelligence, where the same intentions are being shared by you and life. This intelligence knows what is best for your spiritual evolution and the evolution of others and will provide you with all you need to manifest your purpose, as you need it, and when you need it.

Three steps to create a life of purpose

Step 1: Become aware of your intentions.

Your intentions are the main ingredient in creating a life of purpose and promoting attraction. To become aware of your intentions, introspection and presence are necessary. Take a look at your life in the present moment. Do you experience negative feelings such as anger or fear, or discontent around a person or a situation? If the answer is yes, it deserves your attention. Spend as much time as possible in silence, in solitude, in introspection. Be present, and focus on what the moment is here to teach you. Your life now, is a mirror of what it would be in the future, and you have a precious opportunity every moment to make changes that will be carried out later. Without your attention, awareness cannot exist.

Awareness will help you clarify your intentions. Be specific and detailed when you are setting an intention. Life is clear; therefore, it understands clarity. Include everything that you would like to change or attract. Apply the language of abundance, and trust that only those situations and people that contribute to your transformation and spiritual evolution will manifest for you.

Step 2: Acknowledge your talents.

Once you recognize your intentions, acknowledge your talents—this is important in the manifestation of a purpose. Your talents are unique and should be celebrated and shared with others. This is how you co-participate with life in enhancing the collective consciousness. Your talents indicate the direction of your participation.

You know you have a talent when: you are good at doing it, you feel passionate about it, you can spend hours doing it without becoming uninterested, you want to share it with others, and you experience joy, inspiration and creativity as you do it. All these feelings carry positive frequencies and have a positive effect in your life, your relationships, your perceptions, and your health.

Michael Dell, owner of Dell Inc., and one of the richest men on earth, had an interview with the Academy of Achievement where he advised young entrepreneurs on passion. [2] "You've got to be passionate about it. I think people that look for great ideas to make money aren't nearly as successful as those who say, "Okay, what do I really love to do?"

Every time you share your talents with others and express gratitude for them, you attract abundance to your life. Abundance is represented in your capacity to be grateful and your intention to share.

The need to label, segregate, or institute differentiations among people is one of the ways in which we obstruct expansion. It creates separation and limits us from growing or fulfilling our intentions. It is important to honor everything we are, including the so-called "weaknesses." *All* can be instrumental in the creation and manifestation of a purpose. There is no such a thing as a weakness. There are aspects in us that may need attention, can be enhanced or improved, and that is the beauty of life's journey. If everything were flawless, purpose wouldn't exist. We are all moving forward at our own timing, and purpose keeps us moving.

[4] "Your Weakness"

By Author Unknown

This is a story of a ten-year-old boy who decided to study judo despite the fact that he had lost his left arm in a devastating car accident. The boy began lessons with an old Japanese Judo master. The boy was doing well, so he couldn't understand why, after three months of training, the master had taught him only one move. "Sensei," the boy said, "shouldn't I be learning more moves?" "This is the only move you know, but this is the only move you'll ever need to know," the Sensei replied. Not understanding but believing in his teacher, the boy kept training.

Several months later, the Sensei took the boy to his first tournament. The boy surprised himself and easily won his first two matches. The third match proved to be more difficult, but after some time, his opponent became impatient and charged. The boy deftly used his one move to win the match. Still amazed by his success, the boy was now in the finals.

This time, his opponent was bigger, stronger, and more experienced. For a while, the boy appeared to be overmatched. Concerned that the boy might get hurt, the referee called a time out. He was about to stop the match when the Sensei intervened. "No," the Sensei insisted, "let him continue."

Soon after the match resumed, his opponent made a critical mistake: he dropped his guard. Instantly, the boy used his move to pin him. The boy won the match and the tournament.

On the way home, the boy and Sensei reviewed every move in every match. The boy summoned the courage to ask what was really on his mind. "Sensei, how did I win the tournament with only one move?" "You won for two reasons," the Sensei said. "First, you've almost mastered one of the most difficult throws in all of Judo. Second, the only known defense for that move is for your opponent to grab your left arm."

The boy's greatest weakness had become his greatest strength.

Step 3: Your actions must match your intentions.

Action is required for any intention to manifest. To attract and receive, you must "become" first.

A friend of mine wanted to find the love of his life and asked me how he could attract the girl he was looking for. I asked him to think of the traits he most wanted in a girl, and then think if he was cultivating the same traits in his daily life. I explained to him, that in order to attract a person with certain values, or qualities, it is essential to mirror the same behavior we expect from that person. It is necessary to Be, what we want others to Be. If we want kindness, our actions need to be charged with kindness, if we want flexibility, we must be flexible, if we want forgiveness and acceptance, it is vital to exercise compassion and empathy. Actions must be synchronized with intentions.

Realize that you won't always attract what you want or exactly the way you want it. If a person or a situation won't contribute to your well-being, transformation, and spiritual evolution, it won't manifest to you. Spiritual transformation is a purpose, and in this process, life wants to aid you, never harm you. Life is wisdom, it always provides what is best for you.

"Create a purpose" exercise

Step 1: Get clear.

It is vital to be clear on what your intentions are. You might want to initiate change in your life or you might want to attract something new to your life. Whatever it is that you want, express it with clarity.

The main question to get clear on is "What do I want?" Get clear on your intentions, the reasons behind them, and the actions needed to witness their manifestation. When you think of the answers, envision absolutely no limits or obstacles, and concentrate only on the intention.

Some of the questions you can ask are these:

What do I want to change and how?

What do I want to attract and why?

What do I want to become?

Another important part of realizing intentions and creating purpose is awareness of your connection to the world and how your actions affect others. A purpose must be accompanied of actions through which service in the world is expressed.

Ask yourself, "How can I help or be of service to others with this intention?"

Example:

What do I want to change and how?

I want to change my job situation, I want to quit and start my own company.

What do I want to attract and why?

I want to attract money necessary and the right people to aid me in starting my own company.

How can I help others with this intention?

I want to help others by creating jobs. I want to contribute with 10 percent of my profit toward a cause I believe in.

Step 2: Set your intention.

When setting intentions, use specific, detailed statements charged with positive affirmations. Remember, life speaks the language of abundance.

My intention is: _____.

Example:

My intention is to quit my job by the end of this year and start my own consulting business.

My intention is to have $50,000 to pay business expenses and my salary for the first six months.

My intention is to provide high-quality service to my clients.

My intention is to acquire two or more new clients per month and use that income to create more jobs.

My intention is to create a charitable organization that helps endangered whales. I also want to contribute with 10 percent of the monthly profits to an organization that develops grants for education.

Step 3: Recognize your talents and apply them.

Using your talents is instrumental when it comes to setting intentions and attracting what you want. You are the only one who paints, sings, or cooks like you do. Your skills or gifts are signs of your passions and purposes.

My talents are: _____.

Example:

My talents are:

I am great at organizing.

I am a good cook.

I am a people person; I am good at interacting with people.

I am handy.

I love to dive.

I can use my talents toward the manifestation of my intentions.

I can use my _____ to _____.

Example:

I can use my organizational talent toward the creation and development of my new company.

I can use my public relations skill to attract new clients to my company.

I can use my passion for diving to create a charitable organization that helps endangered whales.

Step 4: Initiate action.

Without actions, attraction will not manifest. Set actions that are realistic and that match your intentions, and be consistent with your actions. See each day as an opportunity to move forward. If challenges arrive, they are in your life for a reason. Try to learn from what is being presented to you. Be patient, remembering that everything happens at its perfect timing.

Example:

Intention: My intention is to quit my job by the end of this year to start a consulting business.

Action: I will start a business plan and follow through on specific goals each week toward creating my consulting business.

Intention: My intention is to have $50,000 to pay business expenses and my salary for the first six months.

Action: I will start saving a percentage of my salary toward my business. I will save money by not eating out during the week and eating out once over the weekend.

Action: I will start a freelance consulting job to build a clientele and will save that money for my business.

Action: I will sell my motorcycle.

Intention: My intention is to provide high-quality service to my clients.

Action: When clients approach me, I will listen carefully to their needs and look for practical solutions to improve the situation.

Action: I will treat coworkers with the respect and kindness I want to be treated with.

Intention: My intention is to acquire two or more new clients per month and use that income to create more jobs.

Action: I will start working on a marketing campaign that will help me attract more clients. I will attend meetings at the local Chamber of Commerce to meet people and promote the company.

Intention: My intention is to create a charitable organization that helps endangered whales. I also want to contribute with 10 percent of the monthly profits to an organization that develops grants for education.

Action: I will conduct a research on charitable organizations and will make a plan of action to start my own.

The manifestation of intentions

Traveling is one of my passions. Like many people, Europe was on my list of places I wanted to visit. Traveling to ten European cities in fifteen days didn't appeal to me. My vision of the trip was traveling with flexibility, having the opportunity to choose which places to visit and how long to spend in each one. I also wanted to experience each place's culture and traditions—if possible, by living with locals. I didn't want to spend lots of money but wanted to have lots of experiences. I wanted to be able to rest and not have a schedule or any work-related responsibility. This seemed like a pretentious request when I had little savings, a child to take care of, and a job to maintain.

As if life didn't have enough with this intention, I had another one. For years, I had heard an intuitive voice say to me, "You must write a book." Writing had never been my profession but always something I did with love and enthusiasm. This book was a project that I wanted and was ready to put in motion.

The time for my son to leave the United States, to study in another country for one year was approaching. Again, intuition said, "You can use this year to travel to Europe." As inaccessible as it seemed at that time, I knew to trust my voice within and set the following intention: "I want to travel in Europe for a year with no financial scarcity. I want to be healthy and safe during my trip. I want to attract people who will support this intention before and during the trip. I want to have the time and flexibility to write a book."

I knew that matching actions with my intentions was required, and I started working toward what at the time was a dream. I used my talents as much as I could to facilitate what I needed to prepare for the trip. I had no expectations, but my intentions were clear. I knew if these intentions didn't manifest, it was because they weren't in my best interest, so I showed up to do what I believed was necessary for the intentions to become reality. The rest I left up to life.

During that time, a strong hurricane passed through Florida flooding my condominium. This situation, disguised as a "casualty," allowed me the opportunity to think whether or not I wanted to continue living in my home. I decided to sale the condominium. Through a friend, I met an amazing realtor who, in the midst of a housing market crisis, sold my place within a month. I set up a savings account that I didn't touch for two years, and I sold almost all of my furniture and donated most of my belongings. I moved from a three-bedroom to a one-bedroom apartment to save money, bought little to no clothes for two years, and did extra freelance work to add to my savings. I visited the library every weekend and checked out videos on traveling to get information on the places I wanted to visit. I contacted everyone I knew and told them about this trip in case they knew someone in Europe who could offer a place to stay. People began to provide suggestions and the contact information of their friends in Europe. I was overwhelmed by the support and encouragement that family, friends, and people I didn't even know extended to help me accomplish this dream. The preparation for the trip was fun, and I enjoyed every second of it.

I left the United States in August 2010. During the trip, I met extraordinary people and had amazing experiences. In terms of housing, an aunt and uncle kindly offered their home in Belgium for as long as I needed it. I volunteered in an organic farm in Italy, and on many occasions, strangers, family and friends allowed me to stay in their homes, free of charge.

During the winter, I lived in Belgium. The cold weather allowed me to stay indoors and with plenty of time and my host family's kindness, I was able to complete this book.

Life needs your clarity, willingness, and readiness to communicate back to you what is needed for intention to manifest through you.

When action is initiated from a place of clarity, there is a quality to it that allows life to flow with ease. This quality is charged with four aspects: enthusiasm, flexibility, responsibility, and trust.

The four aspects of quality action

Enthusiasm

Enthusiasm is to life what a condiment is to a dish. Without it, life is just a series of events. Acting with enthusiasm allows you to get through moments that may seem difficult with a sense of smoothness.

Enthusiasm is a source for inspiration, vision, and wonder. When shared with others, it softens your heart and the hearts of those around you. It is contagious, carrying positive energy that expands to others, creating the same effect in them. Actions that are accompanied by enthusiasm communicate aliveness, appreciation, recognition, and alertness.

Flexibility

Life needs your flexibility to flow through you. Without flexibility, you can feel disappointment and frustration when things don't turn out as you expected.

Being flexible when initiating action allows you to adapt in any situation. Life is always changing and your capacity to adapt to these changes allows you to embrace whatever life wants to show you. Life's intention is to ignite transformation and your flexibility will allow this gift to take place.

Responsibility

When action is initiated with a sense of responsibility, you can take ownership for its effect, whatever this might be. Every action has a reaction that causes an effect within you, in others, and in the environment you occupy. I have seen people take credit for an action that produced the results they expected but blamed life, their family, or other factors if their actions produced dissatisfactory results. Taking responsibility for your actions and their effect implies maturity, awareness, strength, and integrity.

Blaming others for your own lack of action, taking credit for actions effectuated by others, or taking action and blaming others for its unexpected outcome promotes dishonesty, weakens your character, and blocks transformation.

Trust

Trust exists when you have the certainty and conviction that life always provides what is best for you.

Life doesn't know negativity, only balance, so its primary purpose is to support that balance within each one of us and within the universe. Every time you initiate action toward the fulfillment of an intention, trust that life is here to support and guide you, never to create suffering or punish you.

Situations arrive to ignite transformation, even when perceived as unfair or negative, their purpose is to strengthen your spirit and promote balance.

Life's expression of balance can be represented in nature. Many people perceive events such as earthquakes, hurricanes, and tsunamis as some kind of mistake or punishment, but life never punishes, only brings about change and always manifests in terms of balance. For humans is hard to grasp the perfection within life's order because our consciousness is covered by layers of attachments causing us to create perceptions from a place of fear, but it is because of situations like these that we are able to witness the love, compassion, capacity of service, and willingness to help others in need. We all hold this capacity within, it is often expressed when a nation shows its people's resilience and strength to move forward after a so called "catastrophe."

Life is ready to co-participate with you, but for purpose and intention to manifest you must be ready as well, trusting that when your intentions come from awareness and your actions are aligned with those intentions your reality will be manifested to mirror life's love, harmony, peace and joy.

Suggestions

Create space for intentions to unfold.

Look for time and space during your day when you can Be in your own company. Spend as much time as possible in silence, in solitude, in introspection. Be present, stay alert, and in that alertness listen to your internal voice.

Make a list of your talents.

Make a list of your talents and write next to each one, ways in which you can share them with others.

Start a journal of "intentions".

Writing helps to clarify your intentions. Start a journal where you can write any intention you have. Be specific and detailed when you are setting an intention. Include anything and everything you would like to change or attract. Apply the language of abundance and trust that only those situations or people that contribute to your spiritual evolution will come into your life. Try not to think or worry about money or anything that may block your intention from unfolding. First it is necessary to get clear on your intentions, the reasons behind them and the actions needed to witness their manifestation. So when you think of the answers, think there are absolutely no limits or obstacles, concentrate only on each intention. Start with general statements and then narrow down to specific intentions.

Set a monthly intention.

Write on a calendar an intention per month, as well as the actions needed to bring about your intention. An example can be strengthening your family relationships by visiting a family member monthly. Every intention is important and valuable, not matter how simple it may seem.

PRACTICE 8

SPIRITUAL RESPONSIBILITY: CREATE YOUR OWN REALITY

Accept your past, honor your present, and create your future.

Gandhi said, "My life is my message." Gandhi's message was, and remains today, a teaching based on principles of non-violence, courage and truth. His actions transcended to change not only the course of a nation but the spirituality of millions of people.

Whether you believe this is your only life or you have ahead of you a multitude of lifetimes to go through, you are the only one responsible for your reality; your actions and choices in the present will create the life you want in the future.

Spiritual responsibility occurs when we take ownership of all we are (our form and our spirit). Our actions then promote spiritual evolution.

When we are spiritually responsible, we understand that who we are, what we say and do creates not only our reality, but also causes an effect on our consciousness and the consciousness of the world.

Alertness is required to identify those parts of ourselves that need transformation. It takes a great deal of courage to look inside. Self-love and compassion are also necessary to initiate change.

Our spiritual essence, which is represented as the light within us, is expressed through *conscious moments*; during these moments we may experience joy, peace, inspiration, compassion, presence, profound love toward oneself and others and a strong sense of balance inwards and outwards. On the other hand, our attachment to human form, which is represented as the absence of light, is expressed through *unconscious moments;* also known as *ego moments*. During these moments, we may experience anger; the need to include or exclude others by labeling, comparing, attacking or judging; feelings of superiority; the need to create drama by being impatient or complaining; resistance in the midst of a situation; the need to gossip or criticize; fear and suffering from an attachment.

Many people yearn to reach consciousness by becoming free from ego, but consciousness, which is also true freedom, is reached through the ego by dissolving it; not by getting rid of it. Trying to get rid of ego can be a manifestation of ego itself when it becomes a means to an end. Ego is not the enemy, it is a signal that is constantly alerting us of patterns that are obstructing our growth and are in need of transformation.

To dissolve ego, we must first recognize it. The three most common ways in which ego manifests through us are: blame of the past, attachment to form and feeling a sense of separation from others and life itself.

As we evolve spiritually, our *conscious moments* increase in frequency. More often than not we stop blaming the past and take responsibility of our actions. We experience detachment from outcomes, form, and people. We feel in common-union (or communion) with life, spirit, nature and all other human beings.

Blaming the past

Questioning how your present would be if something had happened differently in the past will take you to a dead end in your journey toward transformation. "Would have" or "should have" are two futile statements. If something should or would have been, it would be already. Life's intelligence participates by facilitating only what is best for us. When something doesn't manifest, it is often for reasons we don't understand. Our mind tries to explain, analyze and question but life's wisdom cannot be understood, only trusted.

Blaming life for a situation is an easy way to escape from taking ownership of our reality. Life embodies pure consciousness promoting growth—always. Our lack of awareness is the cause of our suffering, and only we are responsible for initiating transformation.

We all have experienced suffering in our past, but our past is also our teacher. The challenging situations we have experienced in the past can serve as reminders of actions we might not want to repeat in the present, or ever. By blaming the past, we avoid taking spiritual responsibility in the present. Dissolution of suffering can be attained through consciousness, but it takes our active participation to make this happen.

To evolve, it is necessary to take action in the present, one action at a time. Blaming the past is easier than owning the present. Change the perception: "life is so much work" to "life is an opportunity for continuous growth." "There was a lot of suffering in my past" to "my past granted me the opportunity to become more aware and conscious." This allows you to view the present as just that: a present.

Every time you experience an unconscious moment and become aware of it, welcome it, and from a place of acceptance, transform it with an action that promotes consciousness.

Attachment to form

Our nature on this physical plane, and one of ego's strongest manifestations, is attachment to form. This often results in suffering when form changes or dissipates. We know we experience detachment when the absence of form doesn't affect our state of peace. For example, it is natural to experience sadness when a loved one departs, but as we read in a previous chapter, there is a difference between sadness and suffering. Our ability to let go in peace determines our state of detachment and therefore our state of consciousness.

It is possible to enjoy everything the world has to offer and obtain freedom from it, all at the same time. How? Understanding that form arrives momentarily, sometimes for short periods and other for longer. Form changes or dissipates at some point or another. When you enjoy something without expectations and allow it to leave when it is time to do so, you can say you are free of it. Ironically, the world is our tool to become free from the world. How perfect!

Sense of separation

Separateness creates a gap between you and others and between you and life. We intensify our sense of separation when we: compare ourselves with others, feel superior or inferior than others, segregate ourselves or others, place people in categories, label, judge or attack, disrespect other people by imposing our opinions or our decisions.

Each one of us is a reflection of life's wholeness, sharing the same qualities: humanity and spirituality; the same rights: joy and freedom; and the same purpose: consciousness. When it comes to consciousness, three elements differ from person to person: timing, readiness, and willingness. Each one of us is ready and willing to evolve, spiritually speaking, at different times, which is why comparing our life with the lives of others is unproductive.

Every life counts, every way is valid, and every soul evolves sooner or later. Respect is one of the most important values to cultivate when it comes to transformation. You are responsible solely for your spiritual evolution—no one else is. No one's evolution is your responsibility either. Honoring everyone's journey and awareness allows life to manifest through all of us with ease, you can learn from the lives of others by observing, without imposing. Action can ignite transformation in others when the purpose behind the action is your personal transformation. Allowing others to be who they want to be, and are ready to be, is an expression of respect and freedom.

If you become aware of instances when you compare yourself with others, judge others, or feel superior, think of the following questions:

Have I ever acted in a similar way?

If I were in the same situation and was that person, how would I have acted?

Compassion and empathy allow for the dissolution of ego created by a sense of separateness. I once read: "If we were compassionate, we wouldn't feel the need to forgive." Your capacity to put yourself "in the shoes of others" allows you to be more forgiving.

Responsibility and your future

Actions derive from your state of awareness and have a powerful effect on everything and everyone around you. They can destroy or create, they can inspire others, they can obstruct or promote growth, but more importantly your actions dictate your reality, they determine the type of life you have and the type of world you inhabit. Your actions create your future, you will harvest then what you cultivate now.

Making the decision to take responsibility for your spiritual transformation implies taking ownership of your decisions and choices made in the past as well as the present. Responsibility requires your active participation—showing up every day and every moment with a positive attitude. When you have a positive attitude toward life, your journey is experienced as a project of love and growth, never as a source of suffering.

Collectively and individually, we must take responsibility of our actions to create an environment of peace, a life of joy, a journey of intention, a healthy body, empowering friendships and loving relationships. This is responsible action.

As mentioned before, your journey is a project of love and growth. When it comes to initiating responsible action, four aspects allow you to navigate through any situation with ease: perseverance, consistency, openness, and strength.

Four aspects to navigate through situations with ease

Perseverance

There is a Chinese proverb that says, "A journey of a thousand miles begins with a single step."

I have seen many people experience frustration when they set a goal or intention and don't see results quickly or as they expected. Transformation doesn't occur overnight, unless you go through a life-changing, mystical experience. Dissolving old patterns and creating new ones takes perseverance.

Patience, dedication, and determination are all aspects of perseverance. Every day, do a little. Every moment, do your best. Continue to show up. No one can make changes for you or take responsibility for your personal awareness. These are your rights and your gifts, and you get to enjoy the peace that comes with transformation.

If an action you took created negativity, own it, and transform it the next time something similar arrives. Negative patterns will begin to dissolve, and you will experience more *conscious moments*, more often.

I know an amazing woman who was in a concentration camp during the Second World War. When I met her, she was ninety-three years old and looked twenty years younger. What struck me the most wasn't her lack of wrinkles: her positive attitude got my attention. Her love toward life was contagious. Despite the suffering she went through during the war, despite the loss of many loved ones, despite the challenges or difficulties, she viewed life as a playground where she had two choices: be positive and enjoy, or complain and suffer. She chose to live each day as if it were her last. At ninety-three, she still drives, dresses up, goes out at night with friends, and simply lives. I asked her what her secret to looking so radiant and healthy was (I knew the answer wasn't going to be a face cream). With a big smile on her face, she said, "Perseverance, I don't give up." She added, "If I am able to go, I go, if I am able to dance, I dance, and I will continue as long as I can."

Consistency

In terms of spirituality, transformation comes about when practices that promote consciousness are done with regularity. To change old patterns and create new habits, consistency is necessary. It has been said that after doing something for twenty-one consecutive days, it becomes a habit. From a spiritual point of view, doing anything with consistency will become part of a life of transformation.

Discipline goes hand in hand with consistency. For example, if having a healthier body is one of your intentions, consistent action in the form of exercise, and good nutrition is necessary to be and feel healthy. It might be required of you to wake up an hour earlier every morning to walk around your neighborhood, or you might attend classes at your local gym. Doing yoga with a friend at her house could be an option. Walk around your office building during your lunch hour. A balanced diet can be part of the equation. With consistency and discipline, you will transform habits of consuming processed food to eating foods that nurture your body. You might be able to bring healthy lunches to work. Another idea could be to take a few products out of your pantry that don't promote health and replace them with products that do.

It may feel like there aren't enough hours in a day to follow through on your responsibilities, never mind taking up a hobby or accomplishing a goal you have had for a long time. It might be necessary to reorganize your priorities to create balance. Setting boundaries is appropriate to allow more time to do the activities that are important to you; then match your actions with those intentions. The quantity is not important. The quality and the consistency of your actions will determine your reality.

A healthier body, a life of simplicity, strong friendships, a clean environment, spiritual transformation—whatever you want to create in your life, if done with consistency, it will become a part of who you are.

Openness

Life is always supporting your spiritual evolution. It communicates in many ways how and when to initiate action to ignite transformation within you.

Without openness, life's possibilities cannot be experienced. A movie, a song, the experiences of another person, a trip, a new friend, or unexpected situations are, *all* ways in which life gives you clues. It sends signs of aspects that are instrumental during your spiritual evolution, and openness allows you to be ready to receive whatever life has to offer. You grant life access and allow its flow to manifest through you.

The greatest obstacle to openness is our need to know and control outcomes. No one knows anything for certain when it comes to life events and outcomes. We like to think that we know what the future will bring. We often assume that we will live for a long time, when death could be around the corner. Thinking that we "know" is an illusion. Life can change course in a second. Openness allows us to move through change with a positive attitude, an attitude of nonresistance, trusting that life is wisdom and pure love.

Strength

It takes strength and courage to move forward, change unhealthy patterns, or get out of your comfort zone. Any action you initiate out of personal intention, or as a result of an unexpected life situation, must be accompanied by two aspects that are deeply connected to strength: trusting the power of your intuition and relinquishing your fear.

We all have an intuition or a "gut feeling." Intuition speaks through your consciousness. It is that voice or feeling that tells you what action to take—or not. Many times it provides you with knowing when to take action. Intuition is always available, but its clarity depends upon your state of awareness. Sometimes intuition shows up as impulse, an inexplicable force within. At times, it seems as if a voice is speaking in the subconscious, and other times, it manifests through a reaction in the body. Noise and distractions prevent intuition from manifesting. Increased moments of presence, silence and solitude allow your intuition to speak to you.

Fear is the voice of the ego, and it speaks through your thoughts. When a thought of an unwanted future event arises, you might feel despair, concern, anxiety, or stress.

To dissolve fear, it is important to understand it. Fear is based on a thought of a past or future event that exists only in your mind, because neither, (past nor future) exist. That is why letting fear dictate your state of Being in the present is futile. Fear evokes feelings that create a high degree of negativity, obstructing spiritual growth and promoting confusion.

Your plans, dreams, intentions, and goals for the future can be created or attracted only from your actions in the present. As you work on your spirituality, you begin to create a different reality for yourself, one based on trust rather than fear. This is strength within. This strength can transform any situation into a work of love, compassion, and peace. This strength has the power to create new outcomes, and transform who you are.

"Creating my reality" exercise

Write "My Reality" on a piece of paper. Write the habits, values, and aspects that you want to cultivate to create the life you want. Below each item, write down the realistic actions that you can initiate in the present. As you begin to take action that supports the type of life you want, awareness will emerge and a new reality will manifest.

Example:

Value: A strong relationship with family members.

Action: Call my family members once a week to catch up with them and see how they are doing.

Action: Go out to dinner with my mother once a week. Take her out to a museum or event once a month.

Initiating action doesn't have to imply hard work. If you are perseverant, consistent, open, and hold the strength to initiate change, you will become an active co-participant with life, and life will flow through you with grace and ease.

We all yearn for a life of quality and balance. We co-exist and aid each other with our actions in creating the world we live in. Only you can decide how you want to make use of the signs, situations or people that arrive in your life.

How our actions affect the world

Spiritual responsibility is essential when creating a different world. The following story is about a monk who wanted to change the world.

"When I was a young man, I wanted to change the world. I found it was difficult to change the world, so I tried to change my nation. When I found I couldn't change the nation, I began to focus on my town. I couldn't change the town, and as an older man, I tried to change my family.

Now, as an old man, I realize that the only thing I can change is myself, and if I had changed myself long ago, I could have made an impact on my family. My family and I could have made an impact on our town. Their impact could have changed the nation, and I could indeed have changed the world."

Responsibility is personal. You cannot change another, and the only way you can introduce change for another is by changing yourself. We spend a lot of time judging, criticizing, worrying about, and observing what others are doing. We also worry about what others might do in the future. Directing that precious energy toward our spiritual evolution will ignite transformation within and, therefore, transform the world.

Suggestions

"Forgiving the past" ceremony.

I find this ceremony to be deeply healing. Choose a day when you are able to have time for self-observation and solitude. Write on small pieces of paper the names of people toward whom you have acted unkindly. Write as well, situations from the past where you experienced loss, guilt or suffering. When you finish, put all the papers together in a small fire pit and burn them. While the paper burns, make an intention to only use those experiences as a source for spiritual transformation and not to create any more suffering in you. Repeat as many positive affirmations as you can think of. For example: "I am peace. Life is wisdom. I am grateful for these lessons. I wish the best for (name of person.)"

Work on detachment.

Choose an object you use often. One that you love or consider you cannot live without. Ask a friend to keep it for a few hours or for a few days. Observe how you feel and imagine your life without it. This exercise helps you to identify your level of attachment to an object and work on your capacity to let go of form with ease.

Practice perseverance.

Choose an activity that you want to do but have been avoiding, such as exercise. Commit to doing it for five consecutive days, then ten, and then a month. Celebrate when you complete each period of time by doing something you like. You can get your friends involved and have a "night out" to celebrate at the end of each period. During this time of celebration, everyone can share their challenges and accomplishments.

Getting out of your comfort zone.

If possible, once a month get out of your comfort zone by doing an activity you have never done before or feel uncomfortable doing, such as going to the movies alone or learning how to install a ceiling fan in your home. These activities help you expand your capacity to adapt to new outcomes and learn something new.

Each one of us travels a unique journey that ultimately arrives at clarity. Life guides us along the way, presenting situations that help us strengthen our spirit, expand our mind, learn from each other, love unconditionally, express gratitude, extend kindness and donate ourselves through service.

The practices presented in this book will support your journey toward clarity. As you welcome simplicity, silence, introspection, self-respect, presence, gratitude, purpose and responsibility to your daily life, your perceptions will change, your actions will be charged with quality and your life will be forever transformed.

It is a privilege to travel this journey and share it with you. I wish you immense peace. I wish you a journey of clarity where your intentions manifest and where every day is a celebration of a life lived in purpose.

BIBLIOGRAPHY

1. *"Generation M2: Media in the Lives of 8-to 18-Year-Olds." Kaiser Family Foundation. 8010. 2010-01-20. 2011-02-01. http://www.kff.org/entmedia/8010.cfm.)*

2. *("Michael Dell Interview." www.achievement.org. 2008-07-03. 2011-03-15. http://www.achievement.org/autodoc/page/del0int-6)*

3. *("Your Weakness." www.inspirational.travellerspoint.com. 2010-11-25. 2011-03-20. http://inspirational.travellerspoint.com/2/)*

ABOUT THE AUTHOR

Ana was born in Mexico City and moved to the United States at the age of nineteen.

During her late twenties and most of her thirties, Ana went through situations that allowed her to take a deep look into herself. Realizing that she wanted to change the course of her journey, she began working toward transformation.

Ana has dedicated time and space to each one of the practices presented in her book for many years, causing a powerful effect in the way she experiences life, as well as a shift in the way she views situations.

Through outward meditation, Ana continues using every situation that arrives in her life as an opportunity to promote growth within, as well as for others in the form of service.

Ana works as an Information Architect and User Experience Designer. She practices yoga, is a song writer and an artist. She lives in Florida with her son.

www.ingramcontent.com/pod-product-compliance
Lightning Source LLC
Chambersburg PA
CBHW060253050426
42448CB00009B/1633